IRONING **MONEY**

A JOURNEY OF FAITH, FAMILY AND FREEDOM FROM ADDICTION

BY DENNIS SCOTT FARMER

"To Dad, now you've got all the answers."

TABLE OF CONTENTS

CHAPTER ONE

The Music of the Spheres

Bottles of Diet Coke lined up like soldiers on top of the fridge. Highball glasses perched in the cabinet, clean and ready. There was plenty of ice in the freezer, too, but no Bacardi. Erica and I finished the last drop of liquor the night before and now swore *no more*. We had both quit our jobs by this point, considering ourselves on a sabbatical from life, agreeing we just needed some time to decompress, get our heads clear, design the life of our dreams, then we'd get back into the rat race, somehow. That's what we told ourselves anyway.

Through the window, I could see where my stepdaughters would ordinarily have waited for the school bus by the roadside in the bright Los Angeles sunshine. I could hear the neighbors' pots and pans rattling as they prepared breakfast. Breakfast—the kind you actually eat—was a distant memory for Erica and me, but all that was going to change. I washed dishes, dried them, and put them away meticulously, perfectly, as I dreamed of the new life we were going to lead starting now. I could hear my in-law family fighting with one another already, in the apartment we now shared with some of them, but I wasn't bothered. Erica and I were getting our lives together despite the fact that we had put ourselves right back into the chaotic lion's den of this Mentone Avenue apartment building.

Normally, the phone would have rung about this time in the morning when the deadbeat father of my wife's youngest daughter Alyssa would call to yell at Erica about "his" daughter. Or he'd drive over and yell through the window or bang on the door at midnight, but he'd gained custody of Alyssa by this point, so at least the bastard had no reason to call us. He'd gotten what he thought he wanted. Plus, no one really knew we were back in Los Angeles. The father of Leila, my older stepdaughter, had taken her away by this point, too, so Erica and I were alone, now, except that we were sharing an apartment with her aunt, uncle, and grandmother.

Taking a woman's child away is a cold thing to do, and Erica was devastated, like she didn't know which end was up, like she'd lost a limb and didn't know how to do basic life functions. If I had any positive role as her husband, I needed to help her get those kids back. Everyone knows courts don't like taking kids away from moms, so all we had to do was get clean, get sober, be the parents those girls deserved, and I knew we'd get them back. We had to. It'd been eternity since I'd seen my wife smile, and that makes a man feel low, indeed.

Erica emptied an ashtray into the garbage. I scrubbed the steel sink until it gleamed. She tried to arrange things neatly in the cramped bedroom that was the only space we could call our own. I opened a kitchen cabinet and realized we didn't have any food but breakfast cereal, so I lined up the boxes perfectly, as if catawampus cereal boxes were the real cause of all our problems.

She tied up a garbage bag. I took it out to our building's dumpster. She mopped the floor. I made the bed. All the while, I couldn't help but be happy because someone nearby was playing my favorite music. I sang along with Mick Jagger ...

Please allow me to introduce myself
I'm a man of wealth and taste
I've been around for a long, long year
Stole many a man's soul and faith
I was 'round when Jesus Christ
Had his moment of doubt and pain
Made damn sure that Pilate
Washed his hands and sealed his fate

The bit about Jesus and Pilate meant nothing to me then, but the classic song reminded me of younger days and freedom and innocence. It made me smile, and I couldn't believe it when the next song the neighbors played was George Strait! Boy those neighbors had incredibly good taste ranging from classic rock to country. It was like they could see into my soul or something. I made a note to go and make friends with them, soon. After all, we were about to become a new couple, an outgoing couple who made friends and were upstanding pillars of the community.

I gathered clothes in the bedroom while Erica scrubbed down the bathroom sink. I noticed none of the pants I picked up off the floor fit me anymore. In fact, I had actually punched new holes in my belt just to keep up my trousers. It was a shame, but I folded them neatly anyway and set them into a drawer, where they would sit and wait for me to put twenty pounds back on. Gathering my shirts into a pile, I wondered how long it had been since I'd actually washed these. No matter. With my newly clear head, I was going to do laundry every day, now! I shoved the shirts into a hamper as I bopped along to *Carrying Your Love with Me.* Then, I couldn't believe what came on, next.

In sleep he sang to me, in dreams he came.
That voice which calls to me...and speaks my name...

Phantom of the Opera? Did these neighbors have a direct line into my brain, or what? It was amazing! I knew all the words and sang them opera-style as I cleaned.

Erica called me a nut. I asked how in the world she could resist singing along, too! She asked, "Sing along to what?"

I assumed she was kidding. The answer was obvious. The neighbors were absolutely blaring the music. My wife and her goofy sense of humor. I just sang louder, and she rolled her eyes. I reminded her this was the first day of the rest of our lives. She told me to stop quoting bumper stickers and pick up the toilet brush. I told her everything was going to change as of today, toilet included. She laughed and agreed. I sang along with Phantom, serenading her, but she didn't seem to appreciate it.

"You're so out of tune, I can't even tell what song you're singing!" she complained. But how could she not know? The music was coming right through the walls.

We took a break from housecleaning, and she said she was "thirsty." I knew what that meant, but I suggested we drink some water instead of the usual. That sounded like what healthy people would do, so we tried it. She gagged. I puked up some green bile. We weren't ready for water, not by the glassful, anyway. My wife was a good sport, though, and suggested it wouldn't be wrong to have Diet Coke without the rum. I agreed to try, but it tasted horrible. I mean, the fact that I could taste it was a problem, in itself.

Water, I had heard, was a medical necessity, even though Erica and I had somehow survived without it for years, except as a mixer. But now, I resolved I would not only drink water—straight, no chaser!—but eat salad, too. What's more, I swore to introduce bread, tomatoes, hamburgers, casseroles, spaghetti, and green beans into our diet … I tried to tempt Erica with these ideas, but just uttering the words actually made both of us ill. We resolved that simply saying the names of foods was enough to start with. If we could do that without dry heaving, it seemed like a start.

Oh yeah, I was going to be a new man. All I needed, I felt, was a good day like today to affirm my resolve not to drink and just fix me. I could fix myself, after all. I didn't need rehab. I'd been to enough rehabs that I felt by now I could do it on my own with the sheer force of my own willpower. Meanwhile, I heard arguing coming from down the hall. Erica's family members were having a go at one another, chattering and fighting as usual, but it didn't get me down!

I reassured Erica this was going to be great. We were going to be better than ever before, in no time! All we needed was dedication! And great music! Luckily, we didn't even need a stereo because our neighbors had the most incredible taste in music, and they played the exact right songs in the perfect order. I felt like I was living inside a karaoke machine! I wondered aloud why I had never before noticed what great taste in music the neighbors had. Or perhaps they had just moved in? Erica looked at me funny.

"What are you talking about?" she asked. "What neighbors?"

"I don't know if they're on the right or left of us, but they have great taste!" I announced. "Maybe they're in the building next door?" I said and looked out the window as if I might suddenly find an Eagles album cover painted there.

She gave me a half smile and said, "Okay. Whatever."

I realized we hadn't ever really talked about music before. Imagine not knowing your own wife's taste in music! I had been so remiss in getting to know her, but things were going to be different, now. I pictured us setting up Spotify playlists together or buying CDs or whatever people do. I actually hadn't kept track of how music worked these days. I'd had my liquid distraction for the past decade or so, but the first thing I was going to do in my sobriety was get caught up on the latest audio technology, I decided. I told her, "From here on out, our lives are going to be filled with music!"

She looked at me like I'd lost my mind, but I was just happy, for once. I wanted her to be happy, too. Sure, we had some problems to solve, but we could do it, together. She smiled in a tired way and said yeah, we'd do it together. She seemed to need some convincing. We went on like this, all day long— cleaning the house, listening to the neighbors' music, resolving to change our lives. We both had the dry heaves a couple of times, but we were undaunted. Getting sober was just a matter of will power, and we were going to do it together.

Eventually, right around the time the girls would have normally come home from school, Erica collapsed on the couch. Throughout the day, I gained energy from the incredible nonstop music that came through the walls, but Erica seemed to be drained by it, by the cleaning, by everything.

She tried drinking more water, eating something small. That didn't go well, but I told her not to give up. We were starting at the bottom, but we'd make it. Maybe just one flake of cereal at a time was the way to do it. She got one crumb down, and we called it a victory.

The gorgeous California sun went down, and, sadly, along with it, the music went away. Erica and I decided to call it a day and went to bed, but I couldn't lie still. I still heard something loud and clear, but it wasn't music anymore, and I was confused. Why had the neighbors stopped playing my favorite tunes? They had kept me in a good mood for so long! Then, there in the bedroom, while I was trying to rest my head, something spoke to me. This time, it wasn't coming through the walls but was, instead, a deep, dark, demonic voice coming from what sounded like hell itself. The voice barked and squealed and told me I should make myself a cocktail and have done with it. It told me being "good" was for assholes. It told me to party and have a good time.

Then, I heard another voice. It might have been an angel or some part of myself—my better half? It spoke rationally and told me *Dennis, stay sober. Be a good boy. You have a wife and kids to take care of. Straighten your life out, Dennis. Toe the line. You can do this.*

Soon, the voice became audible to my ears and was no longer inside my head; meanwhile, the devil argued and laughed at and mocked the angel. The devil had a better grasp on reality, actually, but I told them both to go away… yet the voices got louder. They shouted at one another, then at me. I finally wondered if that music I'd been hearing all day might not have been real. It had been coming from inside my head, just like those voices, all day long. The devil, the angel, the music—it was all part of my withdrawal. Over time, the voices got louder, argued harder. I could hear them as clearly as if they sat on the bed next to me. I hadn't been twenty-four hours yet without a drink and already I was hearing things. Then, I started seeing things. Devils, demonic forces, ungodly things, horrible things, and voices, voices, all urging me to say and do terrible things, trying to destroy my mind (what was left of it). This was made all the more terrifying by the fact that I couldn't manage to keep my eyes closed.

That night, when she heard me screaming and flailing around on the bed, Erica sat up in bed. She then heard me praying. What possessed me to pray at that moment, I still don't know, but I prayed, artlessly, as a last-ditch effort to make the voices stop. Finally, with a sigh and that same sad, tired look on her face, she called an ambulance. There wasn't any other choice left.

I couldn't do this on my own any more than I could fly to the moon. My body had been running for years—to the extent that it was functioning at all—on pure alcohol. Now, I couldn't eat, couldn't drink. I had been through withdrawals before, but not without a suite of drugs to counteract the effects. I had no idea what this would be like without being in a detox facility. In fact, the residual alcohol in my system had been the very thing that gave me the confidence to quit drinking. Now that it was all out of my system, I faced more than just the tiredness, nausea, and agitation of a typical physical detox; I faced a crisis of the soul that demanded I face God with all my transgressions. In so doing, I confronted the devil … perhaps the actual devil or perhaps the one inside me that drove me to live the way I did. Nonetheless, it was as close to hell as I ever hope to get.

They gave me something at the hospital to make the demon go away, and I eased my conscience by saying it was one big hallucination, but part of me knew it really wasn't. That devil speaking to me may have been more real than the apartment I had just cleaned. It may, in fact, have been the only true reality I had ever faced in my life.

Oh, Erica and I returned to drinking, of course. One trip to the emergency room and my resolve was toast. But I never forgot that devil voice and the day-long auditory hallucination that preceded it. It was God taunting me with my favorite music, then turning the tables and confronting me with the deepest darkness in my soul. It would be a long time before I returned to face that devil, but I knew one thing: those demon and angel voices were real, and the choice they presented would have to be made, sooner or later.

CHAPTER TWO

Small Town Gossip

A breeze riffled my bedroom windows as I lay there, staring at the ceiling. I cherished these quiet evening moments, crickets chirping, moonlight streaming over the rooftops. I could smell the farmland just a few miles outside of town. Peaceful hours were few and far between throughout the nineties, when I was a teen, and I didn't want to sleep through this one. The summer evening was pleasantly cool. Nobody was slamming things around. The night was mine. My brain could reset. But then I heard a car engine rumbling close, closer, and finally I knew it was Dad. I heard the garage door go up with its unique hum and rattle. My clock radio said it was a little after two in the morning. So much for my moment of reverie.

Clang! Clang! Clang! went the wildly swinging belts on the rack attached to the back my parents' bedroom door. Upon hearing the garage door, Mom had sprung out of bed like a jack in the box and flung the door open. The carpet did little to muffle her stomping as she pounded out of the bedroom, down the hall, and onto the hardwood of the living room entryway, where her familiar angry trudge took on the innocent pitter-pat of bare feet. But Mom wasn't headed for the front door. The detached garage, Dad's domain, was out the back, entered through the alley via car or through the yard, on foot. So, she pivoted and galumphed across the living room carpet. You'd think my mother would have weighed four hundred pounds by the heaviness of her footfalls, but at 5'2" she probably topped out at 140. I guess she put about two hundred and sixty pounds worth of anger into each soft but ominous floof that took her across the rust-colored shag and finally to the kitchen linoleum, where her foundation-shaking footfalls were accompanied by the rattle of dishes in the cupboards and cutlery in drawers. Once I heard her stomp across the linoleum, I knew … there was no turning back.

Then, I heard the squeak of the back door hinges just prior to the smash of the door crashing into the wall where there used to be one of those spring things that prevent doors from crashing into walls before it was destroyed by years of rage-fueled evenings just like this one.

Smash! went the kitchen door, which made it sound like innumerable household items were crashing from their proper places. She left an apocalypse in her wake. It was all because my mother still fancied we had the potential to be normal people with bedtimes and jobs and good grades in school and a husband that didn't get thrown in jail now and then. I suppose it's a mother's right to fantasize about a life not lived in abject desperation. As for me, I had no sense of which of my parents was right or wrong. I loved them both but kept that fact to myself. To me, since I'd been about twelve, life outside of school was just a lot of screaming. Before that, Dad used to hold down a job as a carpet layer in his family business. I didn't know what happened or when, exactly, but Dad wasn't himself, anymore. Hearing Mom's angry footfalls, I braced myself.

Mom's shutting of the kitchen door was followed, predictably, by an eerie silence as she padded down our concrete walk. The silence was broken only by the squeaky door into the garage—sounds that now came to me via my open window. There, she screamed at Dad in words I couldn't make out, but they probably had something to do with his long-term absence, lack of money, lack of good sense, lack of law-abiding decency, and general disreputable coming-home-at-two-a.m. nature. But this time, I could tell there was something else, as her volume and tone seemed even angrier than usual, if that was possible.

At this point, I was curious— dangerously so. Mom's subsequent screaming went up a decibel. I heard a car door slam, which meant Dad had exited the car. He yelled back at her, but to no avail. I was curious as to what was going on tonight that was different from most nights. So, since I'd gone to sleep in my basketball shorts, I didn't hesitate to pop out of bed and follow Mom's trajectory, barefoot, shirtless, through the house, out the kitchen door, across the sidewalk, and into the garage, where I witnessed the whole scene.

When I got to the garage, I realized Dad had brought a woman in the car. There was no telling what role she played in Dad's life, but I doubted she was his accountant. Her presence was a new twist. I wasn't ever sure if Dad was faithful to Mom, but the possibility that he wasn't just seemed obvious, what with his weeks-long absences. By this point, though, Dad had gotten back in the car and was trying to take off, down the alley. Mom was red-faced with rage. I didn't see much of the woman in the passenger seat except to acknowledge she was indeed there, because my mother was screaming directly at her, now, through a window that was almost but not completely rolled up.

Dad's attempt to drive away enraged my mother further, so she leapt on the side of the car, where her bare feet or knees must have found purchase on some indentation in the door and her fingers clutched the window through the gap at the top of it. She clung to the thing like a pajama-clad gargoyle and rode the passenger door, face against the window, just shrieking, as Dad tried to get the car up to speed. I ran after them, yelling at Mom to jump off. I didn't know if Dad was going to speed up, or what. Before he made it to the end of the alley, though, Mom finally dropped to the ground, and he sped away.

Sixteen or so at the time, my main worry was whether or not the neighbors had seen or, more likely, heard. I covered my shame with bravado, as usual. Another of my coping techniques was to milk my bad home life for sympathy from girls. It worked, so that's looking on the bright side.

I hadn't started drinking, yet, and when I would, a year or so later, I'd discover I was great at it. I could drink everyone else under the table, feel fantastic all the while, and never get a hangover. I didn't think of drinking as self-medicating, nor did I think of myself as depressed or disadvantaged, at all. What I thought, actually, was that the concerned people in my town who occasionally tried to help me, give me someone to talk to, and provide general guidance were busybodies who should keep their minds on their own problems.

For instance, at some point shortly after this incident or one like it, my high school principal pulled me out of class. I thought I was in trouble for something, but he said no. In fact, he offered me some chips, a soda, stuff like that, and asked if everything was okay at home.

What was I going to do? Tell him my father was inexplicably gone for weeks at a time and my mother supported the family on poverty wages earned by (ironically) doing office admin support for the very same school district from which she had failed to graduate because of getting pregnant with me?

In fact, the only reason the four of us weren't living under a bridge was because when my parents failed many times in a row to make their mortgage payments, my mother's now-estranged parents took over the house payments so we could stay there. But my grandparents (Papa and Nana) made it clear Mom and Dad only got to live there because of my sister and me. It wasn't his own daughter Papa hated, but the husband who had impregnated her at fifteen and reduced her once-full-of-promise life to that of a rage-filled, car-window-clinging banshee. Add to that the fact that during my first year of life, while Mom was pregnant with my sister, Dad got himself thrown in jail. Even before all that, though, my grandparents hadn't been a fan of Dad. After all, he'd been a shiftless foster care kid. So, there were reasons Papa didn't think Dad was good enough for his properly raised daughter … but what did any of that matter, now?

Even in the midst of all this strife, Mom stubbornly stood by Dad, which drove her comparatively affluent father into such a state that my parents forbade me from talking to him or Nana, either. So … was I going to tell all that to my school principal? What good would it do? Besides, the chance this information would leak out into the general public, small towns being what they are, was practically 100%.

Wasn't the outwardly obvious aspect of my life embarrassing enough, without all the background details? Didn't the people in this town have enough Farmer family gossip to satisfy their curiosity? I didn't see, at that age, how "having someone to talk to" could have made a difference. In retrospect, though, I realize that the typical teenage fear of public humiliation probably stops a lot of kids like me from accepting help that's offered. I got decent grades, after all, at least when I tried. School came relatively easy to me, and I got bored just as easily. I played sports, was in band, and had a lot of friends, too. I thought I was fine and told the principal so. I was, however, confused by the sadness in his eyes. After all, he knew where a childhood like mine could lead, but I didn't.

A few other moments, where I fielded similar inquiries from my teachers, stand out in my memory. On another occasion, I was called from class to report to the music room, even though it wasn't time for band class. There, my music teacher gave me a new trumpet recently purchased for me by my Papa and Nana. They had feared my parents wouldn't allow me to accept it, or worse, might destroy it, so they had arranged for my teacher to present it in this safe location. Thus, it would remain safeguarded in the band room, for years. When my Dad did finally find out about the purchase he threatened to "wrap it around a tree," so perhaps those fears of destruction were warranted, after all.

The way I thought about my life, at that age, was that its trajectory was going to be just like everyone else's in my small town: school, maybe college, work, then marriage, kids, retirement, and death. What else was there to life? You go through the motions. I never dreamed I'd act the least bit like my parents and couldn't imagine I'd actually end up even worse. I planned to get my own apartment after high school, as soon as humanly possible, find a nice girl, fall in love, settle down, and raise my children right. How hard could it be?

CHAPTER THREE

Moments with Dad

We used to have both a ping pong table and a pool table. One lived in the detached garage and the other, on the enclosed back porch. They'd frequently change places with each other. Dad probably got these in trade for some nefarious activity or just acquired them through his vast network of "connections," but anyway, they led to Dad and me having some sort-of meaningful moments, now and then.

Sometimes Dad would come home late at night, just like a teenager. Nobody asked where he'd been or what he'd been up to. None of us really wanted to know, to tell the truth. He'd show up at and disappear from our house for inexplicable reasons. Sometimes the night would be pleasant, crickets would be chirping, and I'd be up, just grabbing a late-night snack or something. Dad would come home, and something about the moment and the stillness of the night, and how we were alone together would lead to us playing a game of ping-pong or shooting pool together. Meanwhile, he'd try to talk to me, but he wasn't good at it. I could see him struggling to figure out how to talk to a teenaged son. I couldn't help him, though. I didn't know what to say, either. The best we could do was shoot the breeze— "How's school? Got a girlfriend?"— that kind of thing. Still, those nights were meaningful for me. I only recall a handful of them, but when you're a kid, even five minutes spent with a parent, under the right conditions, can make a memory that sticks forever. That's how it was with Dad.

I'm sure he wished he could get through to me in those moments, tell me something about himself, give me some kind of advice for life, or at least express his love. But he didn't say anything special. There was advice, always plenty of advice, but it annoyed me and fell on deaf ears. In those moments, it wasn't anything he said, but just the fact of his trying that touched me. My mother, of course, tried and succeeded to communicate with me. She raised me. She carried almost the full burden of that upon herself. So, it might be a bit odd for me to say that I was touched by my father's feeble attempts to reach me, but when you can see someone really struggling and being somehow blocked by their own fragile mind, it's touching. It really is.

When I got into drinking, later in high school, I never told Dad. I didn't keep it a secret. It just never came up. He never warned me about alcoholism in the family, and I wouldn't have listened anyway. At that point, I didn't consider drinking a problem at all, but rather a great mechanism for greasing the skids of any social situation, making me more charming to girls, and shutting down all moral arguments against doing something that would otherwise be considered wrong. So, Dad didn't exactly advise me or guide me, but those moments we sometimes had, late at night, just playing a game, being together, struggling to try to be some version of a father and son, they were our way of saying I love you.

CHAPTER FOUR

Grandpa Farmer's Funeral

When Grandpa Farmer, who was Dad's grandfather and my great-grandfather, died, in 1984, our family attended the graveside service. I hadn't known the man well. I was too young when he died. Dad, however, had always had an affection and a respect for Grandpa Farmer. He even lived with his grandparents for a short time in-between foster homes. Despite his respect for Grandpa Farmer, it also wasn't lost on Dad that he had living grandparents the whole time he was being shuffled from foster home to foster home, so his respect for the man was tinged with doubt and confusion.

My Dad's name was Orville, and his mother died of a heart attack at just thirty-seven years old, when he was five. Some years later, Dad's father Martin, who was a raging alcoholic, ended up doing a decade of hard time for manslaughter. So there was Orville, the youngest boy, with his two brothers Bill and Danny and his sister Marlene, the youngest of them all, with a dead mother and a father in prison. Most of them had been born when their parents were still very young, so Dad and his siblings had the same situation as me, where you have grands and great-grands and great-great-grands still alive. Obviously, having teenage parents has its drawbacks, but having a huge network of relatives is one interesting advantage. One would have hoped that in and among all those relations, someone would have stepped forward when Dad and his siblings were left alone.

Interestingly, their Grandpa Farmer was a Pentecostal Assembly-of-God preacher, of all things. A man of God. But he let Dad and his siblings go into foster care— not exactly the kind of life that leads one to fulfill one's highest potential. Their uncles, aunts, and older half-siblings all failed to take them in, too, for reasons still unspoken-of in the family. I mean, how much trouble could they have been? I still don't know why they were abandoned like that. In fact, I don't think anyone alive now remembers the reason. If they do, the story has been sugarcoated too many times to even resemble the truth. Rest assured, however, every relative has his or her own version of the story. So, the state placed Dad, Bill, and Marlene, who were little kids in the single digits, into the foster care system. Thus, what was left of Dad's immediate family was broken up into different homes and raised by different foster parents—all except for Danny, the oldest brother, who I knew as "Uncle Smokey." He was old enough, when child services came around, to split for parts unknown, and that's exactly what he did.

My whole life, everyone in the town of Shafter, California, knew this part of the Farmer family story. Ours wasn't the kind of town where everyone is from a generations-long string of degenerate ne'er-do-wells. Not at all. Most folks were normal. Then … there were the Farmers.

Dad had a lot of resentment against his own father and grandparents and uncles and aunts and great-uncles and great-aunts for declining to care for him and his siblings in their hour of need. A man could spend the rest of his life wondering what he had done as a boy to deserve neglect from such an extensive network of elders. In some respects, Dad did. I mean, how does a man forgive a thing like that? It's hard to do without spiritual guidance at the highest level. Dad never had anything like that, so his bitterness grew over the years. He was angry, resentful, vengeful, even. Deep down, none of that resentment was toward Mom, my sister Janee, or me, but we caught the brunt of it, anyway.

For what it's worth, I did meet Grandma and Grandpa Farmer a few times before they died, and they seemed wonderful, honest, and genuine.

I'm sure life changed them a lot after they made the fateful decision not to take in their grandkids. Maybe they even regretted it. I'll never know.

Out of the four of them, only Dad's brother Smokey seemed more badly impacted by their youth than my father was. Perhaps avoiding foster care hadn't been a great idea after all, as Smokey would eventually become a homeless addict living as a hermit, either on the side of a mountain or in the desert. The stories vary. Wherever it was, Smokey came to deaths doorstep there, alone. Dad was able to get him to a hospital at the very end, so his last day was with family. Dad's brother Bill, on the other hand, put his nose to the grindstone and worked hard all his life up to retirement. On occasion, though, I heard Dad and Uncle Bill speak about their past, and I got the impression Bill was just as unhappy as Dad. Their sister Marlene had a happy life, though, married to the same guy for forty plus years. Deep down, though, I'm sure she battled (and may continue to battle) her own demons. Of all the kids, she'd been the most fortunate in foster care, being raised by the same family from almost the very beginning. My grandfather actually had more kids than the four of them, though. Dad had half-siblings sprinkled all over, whom he knew to varying degrees. The stories I hear about them present a range of vocations from pauper to preacher.

Some might blame Dad's family for giving him psychological scars. Others might blame the devil, saying it got into him as a kid and couldn't be exorcised. Then there are those who think certain people are just "born bad" through a trick of fate. How people turn out (me included) is a complicated issue, and I have my own opinions on it, but I'll get back to that.

What I know now is that my great-grandfather and great-grandmother Farmer raised Dad's father (who was apparently bad from the start), my Great Aunt Pauline (who got married half a dozen times and had a bunch of kids all over the place), and my Great Aunt Ruenell (who is still alive and wouldn't say a cross word about anyone). This, I believe, is why nobody really knows our family history, because all the words to be said are, apparently, cross ones, and the people who know the truth ain't talking.

I do, however, know that sometime after being released from prison, Dad's father Martin showed up again. By then, Dad was out of high school, and I might have even been born. The interaction that ensued would haunt Dad his entire life. Despite being an absentee father and a convicted felon, Martin saw Dad wearing cut-off jean shorts and long hair (It was the seventies, after all) and my grandfather lit into Dad about his looks and comportment. Thing was, Dad, by this point, had a life and a job and didn't relish being told off by a convicted felon no matter who he was, so the two of them got into a knock-down, drag-out fist fight right in front of everyone. That was the last time they ever saw each other.

Shortly after that incident, Martin moved to Texas, where one evening, he got shit-faced at a bar, attempted to take a shortcut home by jogging across a busy highway, and was struck and killed by a car. At least, that's the generally accepted story of his death that most of the family seems to be sticking to.

So there we were, at Grandpa Farmer's funeral—an elaborate Pentecostal affair involving scripture readings and hymns and a casket viewing and a receiving line. The works. Dad was dressed to the nines, as well as a working man can be. He was always very concerned about appearances, my dad, to the point where he had ironed his suit, shirt, tie, and money for the occasion of the funeral of a man he deeply respected but did not understand. Dad would have done that for any occasion, though. Especially the money. No matter how ill-gotten his gains might be, if Dad had dollar bills in his wallet, they were crisp as potato chips, courtesy of General Electric's 1200-watt mid-sized steam iron with stainless steel soleplate, ergonomic grip, and auto-shut-off feature. Hallelujah. It was a habit he picked up from his own father. The money-ironing was just one aspect of Dad's overall concern about keeping up appearances and being respected. Any time Janee and I were in public with him, he required us to behave with perfect manners and composure. Thus it was at Grandpa Farmer's funeral, when our family got back in the car—a 1979 Camaro, as I recall—Dad suddenly reached into the back seat and smacked the shit out of me. After a period of confusing silence, he told me it was for chewing gum too loud during the service. Punishment and then explanation was usually the order, which led to some intense resentment that built up over the years. But Dad thought he was doing the right thing that day by demanding respect for the family. He felt he was holding me accountable as a good father should. Smacking me was exactly what his own father would have done, wallet full of ironed money and all.

Yeah, my father was no prince, but if you look at it a different way, he did, to some degree, improve the family brand. After all, his own father used to bring drunk buddies home from the bar, make his sons fight with each other, and they'd place bets on them. Dad was nothing like that.

CHAPTER FIVE

Papa's Diesel Pickup

I remember when I was maybe 10 or 12, Mom sending me over to the house of her parents, my Nana and Papa, to get money for the light bill. After all, how could they turn down a request from their first-born grandchild? But my grandparents were not charmed by this maneuver. When I was younger, Dad had supported the family pretty well, but right around this point, something went haywire with Dad. His demons began to surface, and he just couldn't toe the line, anymore. Nana and Papa didn't appreciate Dad's inability to support his own kids, and arguments ensued, causing resentments to build. Things were said that couldn't be taken back. Nana and Papa took over the mortgage payments on our home to keep a roof over their grandchildrens' heads, but by the time I was in high school, my parents and maternal grandparents had severed all ties but that one. Further stress was added when Nana and Papa made it clear they planned to kick both my parents out of the house they now owned as soon as Janee and I left home, which we both hoped to do with the utmost alacrity.

I lived three blocks from the high school, but I remember how, while walking to school, I'd hear the sound of Papa's diesel truck about a block from home. As soon as I was out of sight of my house, he'd cruise around the corner, stop long enough for me to climb in, and we'd drive to school together, usually without saying much. He used to give me a little bag of candy to throw in my locker "for emergencies," as well as a couple bucks for lunch. It wasn't anything he said that made us feel close, it was just the way he always showed up. Plus, there's only so much you can cover in a two-block trip.

Oh, sure, Dad chewed my ass out whenever he was out on the street for some reason and saw Papa pick me up. We weren't allowed to talk, me and Papa, but that didn't bother us. Getting yelled at by Dad, after all, wasn't much of a punishment. It was yelling and screaming all the time at my house, anyway.

The only other kid who knew about the any of my woes was Brad Wiedmann. Or, at least he knew more of the story than most. Brad and I had an unusual basis to our friendship: we were born on the same day, the same year, and were growing up just a few blocks from each other. We played sports together, had gone to every grade since kindergarten together, and, during my last year of high school, drank together, too. This was the only place where we were different, as I could drink anyone under the table and Brad constantly sought to match me drink for drink. No chance! Brad and I had another friend, too, named Zeb Smith, and we were the three musketeers for many years, all the way up until we graduated, got married, and life took over.

When we were kids, though, Brad, Zeb, and I always had each other. By contrast, Brad came from a family that had owned the local pharmacy for nearly a hundred years and was incredibly stable. Zeb's life was pretty normal, too. Of course, that's just an assumption made in my youth. After all, who was I to make judgment on what was "normal?" I didn't talk much about my home life with them. Didn't want to. I assumed that, like folks most in town, they knew. I appreciated them for never making me talk about it. I wanted to get the hell out of that house as soon as possible and not think or talk about it, at all. I was a kid in high school, after all, and the world was full of interesting places to explore and girls to seduce. Why dwell?

CHAPTER SIX

Farmer Family History

"**S**on!" Dad called out as soon as I got home from school. "Get in the car!"

I had barely had time to set down my bookbag. He was racing around the house like a maniac.

"That's it!" he added. "We've been robbed! We're going to the cops!"

Throughout my childhood, the cops were at our house a lot. Dad wasn't any type of big-time criminal, but he dabbled in drugs, I think— using them, anyway. I heard him be accused of having, or perhaps dealing in, stolen property and other penny-ante crimes. In our town, Shafter, there were only about 6,000 people with maybe ten police officers to look after them, so, once someone like Dad got on their radar, he couldn't hide much. For me, coming home from school to find cop cars either in the alley by the garage or in front of the house— their red and blue flashing lights bouncing around like carnival signs— was not an uncommon occurrence.

So, to hear Dad tell me he was actually going to *look for* the cops ... this was a new one on me. I can't even guess, now, what had been stolen, but I may have known at the time. So, I got in the car and off we drove. A ways down the road, as luck would have it, we passed a cop car, and Dad stuck his hand out the window and waved like someone in a dire emergency.

The cop pulled over and so did we. Dad jumped out of the car and excitedly spoke to the cop by the side of the road, waving his arms and gesturing with a sense of frustration, clearly implying he was the victim of a great injustice.

The officer nodded sagely. He had a look as if deep in thought. "Tell you what," he said. "Why don't you head back to your house, and I'll follow you there and take a full report."

Dad agreed, and we headed home again with the officer close behind. No sooner did we arrive at the house than the officer walked up and told Dad, "Turn around and put your hands behind your back. You know the drill." Then he turned to me, saying, "You too."

Turns out, the cop had actually been on his way to our house when Dad flagged him down. He had a warrant to search our house for drugs. While he was putting the handcuffs on us, the rest of the police department arrived on the scene; meanwhile, Dad and I stood there like confused idiots. I don't recall, but I think whatever had been stolen was probably what the cop was looking for. He had no more luck finding it than Dad had, so Dad didn't go to jail that day.

My high school graduation was in June of that same year. Mom and Janee came, naturally, but I knew Dad wouldn't make it, as he was in jail for something, again. Interestingly, Dad seldom missed the big events of my and my sister's lives. He usually remembered at the last minute and managed to pull himself together in time to show up before it was too late. He even coached Janee's softball teams back in elementary school and junior high, and always made it to the games, so he wasn't an absent father … but he wasn't what you'd call present, either. So, him missing my high school graduation was a pretty big deal. He didn't typically miss things like that. I'm sure Mom was disappointed in him, but, true to form, she never mouthed a bad word about him to us kids. Yet, as if by a miracle, Dad actually showed up to my graduation!

I don't recall now if I found out before, during, or after the ceremony, but I know for sure that he was there. In fact, later, I found out the local judge had let him out of jail just for my graduation. A cop came along a day or two later and picked him up again, of course. The judge and the police and everyone knew our family and had, I guess, a little bit of sympathy for us. It was a small town, and people cared. They really did. Those little ceremonial moments in life meant a lot to all of us.

After graduation, my Papa, who owned some real estate, helped me make an easy transition to adult life by setting me up with a little house of my own. In that last year or so of high school, Brad and Zeb and I had discovered drinking, and for me it was Heaven. All it took was one drink for me to feel the stress of my life wash away like sand being smoothed over by the tide. Alcohol was, to me, an absolute panacea. Now on my own, I delivered pizza all day and drank Boone's Strawberry Hill wine all night, and it seemed like life couldn't get any better.

Even a slight buzz made me incredibly relaxed, like nothing I'd ever felt before. Over time, I realized drinking even more made me feel even better, so I saw no reason not to enjoy this magical elixir to the fullest extent. Among eighteen-year-old guys, it wasn't hard to find drinking companions, so I threw parties all the time. Life in those first years after high school seemed easy and great. In fact, I wondered at how and why adults had so much ambition, worked so hard, stressed out so much, when all it took to make me happy was enough money to keep my fridge stocked with food (I already got pizza on discount) and my cupboards full of Boone's Strawberry Hill. In fact, I was so unashamed of my new lifestyle I used the bottles to decorate the house. My empties lined the shelves in every room.

It did occur to me that I should "make something of myself" for some reason, so I enrolled at the local community college, several times actually, but I just could never make myself go to class. I had been a reasonably good student in high school, but I wasn't goal directed. I had no sense of what a college degree could get you, no idea that a person could simply name a profession, study for it, and then get a job in that once you had a degree. Bookkeeper. Engineer. Architect. Lawyer. Plumber. Auto mechanic. Administrative assistant. Businessman. Zookeeper. Archeologist. Astronaut. Literally anything.

When you're a teen, if you're willing to work hard and mortgage your life to student loans, you have those choices (if you know about them). You can pick a path and take it. But I'd never met those types of adults.

My mother got her GED while I was in high school, and I remember being really proud of her for that. Mom was smart and had only dropped out of high school to have me, after all. But she certainly never went to college or had anything I'd call a *profession*. In retrospect, I can see how angry my Papa had been to see her "throw her future away" on having me and Janee and marrying Dad. But, of course, Papa loved me and my sister, even though Mom and Dad had officially invited him to take a hike. On the part of my Nana and Papa, the feeling was mutual, so, throughout childhood, us kids were the only connection left between our parents and Mom's parents.

During those heady years of being a teenager on my own, I had a car that I made payments on … sometimes. Financial discipline wasn't a skill I had acquired, yet, and neither was drinking discipline. I knew nothing about how much alcohol was safe to drink or when to stop. For instance, I didn't even know not to get behind the wheel of a car. There were enough public service messages about drunk driving out there that I definitely should have known, but I guess I thought those didn't apply to me. Certainly, no adult in my life had ever pulled me aside and given me a stern lecture about it. No partier I knew had ever given his car keys to someone else and asked, "Can you drive me home? I'm too drunk." We were teens, and we were invincible, and drinking was about the happiest I had ever been, so how could it be wrong? Small town life seemed to offer nothing but the obligation to work and the option to party, so, I reasoned, why wouldn't you?

When I drank, I never showed signs of being drunk. That's how I always drank my friends under the table. Nobody ever stopped me from drinking as much as I wanted. I was the life of every party, and there were simply no consequences. Sure, some people couldn't hold their liquor. They threw up or became violent and belligerent. How embarrassing for them. Not me. When drunk, I was just myself, only better and happier in every way.

Of course, some drunk evenings were superior to others. The good ones were so ecstatic, so euphoric, in fact, that I began a habit of "chasing the high." I wondered—if last night's party was so great, why wasn't tonight's party just as good? Should I drink more to get that same euphoric feeling? In truth, I now know there's no telling why some drunk evenings are better than others. Being drunk is almost like painting a picture or playing an instrument, I suppose—sometimes you're *inspired*, but other times you're just kind of doing it because it's what you do. So… you chase the high.

I never dated sober, either. I mean, if drinking relaxed me, then it made me more likeable, didn't it? I was pretty comfortable around women, but I was no playboy. I guess I was what you'd call a serial monogamist. I'd pick a lady and stick with her until things fell apart or one of us met someone else. As long as there was a party going on, I could be a pretty easy-going guy to hang around with, so I was seldom lonely.

My sister Janee is less than a year younger than me. You could say we're true "Irish twins." But after I moved out, we drifted apart somewhat. She used to come to my parties sometimes, or use my house as a place to meet up with her friends, which was fine with me, but I never returned to my parents' house. Not once. I needed a break from Mom and Dad.

Janee, on the other hand, was either incredibly naive or irrationally loyal, and I'm still not sure if this aspect of her nature was a deficit or asset. She defended our father at every turn, no matter what he did or said, no matter if he was in jail, off with some woman, or getting caught trying to fence allegedly stolen property. Mom was the same way. She could say anything she wanted about (or to) Dad but nobody else had better, including me. The madness and utter dishonesty of it all drove me insane. So, while a life of pizza delivery and partying might not sound terrifically enlightened, it was paradise just to be out of my parents' house and proving I could survive without them.

Right around the time I gave my heart to Bacardi Gold, Janee gave hers to a serious boyfriend named Tony. So, during her senior year in high school, my sister and I crossed paths now and then, but our lives were developing in different directions. When she graduated, she and Tony married and ran off to Texas so he could work in the oil fields. She didn't come back to California until she was pregnant with her first child. The two of them made it work, had three kids, and, over time, bought progressively bigger houses. I guess you could say they were successful, and Janee never really said anything indicating she had any damage from the way we grew up. For instance, for me, being asked not to associate with my grandfather had been a terrible, heart-wrenching issue, but it wasn't for Janee. She had taken the side of Mom and Dad without any trouble at all.

CHAPTER SEVEN

Two Weddings

In those post-high-school years, nobody could accuse me of being ambitious. I could always find someone to hire me to do some kind of menial thing, nothing very challenging, that would pay my basic expenses and booze money, and I was fine with that. I was even able to get into more responsible positions through my sheer ability to talk myself into them. Then, eventually, I applied for work with the California Department of Corrections—ironically, the very prison system where my dad's father Martin had found a "home," such as it was. At one point, my own father would take a short, state-sponsored vacation with the Dept. of Corrections, as well. I got the job, and it quite nicely facilitated my life of random travel, partying, serial monogamy, and general shiftlessness.

This was a great gig for a guy like me because it was almost impossible to get fired, didn't require a lot of thought (or people skills, for that matter), and if I wanted to get transferred to a different location, it was quite easy to do. Also, I discovered, the social scene in the Department of Corrections was as incestuous as it could get.

People that worked there were always dating and marrying one another and breaking up and divorcing, then going on to date other people that worked there. The place was a nest of snakes, but a nest where it was easy to meet women. Just as I never thought I'd become like my parents, I never thought I'd become one of those vipers, either.

Watching these people hop from one partner to another within the same department without missing a beat made my head spin. There was no shame at all. The Department of Corrections was a world unto itself, and the system was structured such that I could easily get transferred to a different location whenever I wanted.

My exodus from the family home at seventeen had a two-fold effect. I left to start my own life, but in doing so, I actually put my parents in peril. My grandfather, who owned my childhood home, had told them quite seriously that he'd paid the mortgage on the house for his grandchildren, and his estranged daughter and her shiftless husband were not welcome to live there once the kids were out on their own. Janee hit the bricks a year after me, at which point Mom and Dad were suddenly evicted and found themselves wandering.

At that point, Dad disappeared, as usual, so I let Mom secretly move into the house where I lived, which was owned by my Papa. Eventually, I confessed this to Pap. He was okay with it, but the rule was that my father could not, under any circumstances, move in. Well, soon enough, Dad showed up, too. At first, he only crashed now and then in-between nightly forays to the homes of his friends or other "associates" and whatnot, but eventually he decided to stick around. There wasn't much I could do about it.

I didn't want to hang around for the drama that was I assumed would ensue, so I told my grandfather I was moving. This would become something I did regularly—just move to a new place to see what it was like.

So, I moved away from my parents for the second time, then told Papa that Mom and Dad were in the house together. I don't recall if the information was coerced from me or if I gave it willingly. I do vaguely recall an argument with Mom and Dad that may have prompted my "outing" of them. Without the least hesitation, Grandpa evicted them as if they were strangers— there was certainly no love lost.

Mom and Dad ended up in an apartment somewhere in the nearby town of Bakersfield. The two of them always landed on their feet, mostly due to Mom's continual employment. They stayed together through it all. I don't know why or how, but they did.

Just prior to my new career at the Department of Corrections, I met a lady named Ritina. At the time, I was still involved in one of the classic serial monogamy situations I considered a "relationship;" nonetheless, Ritina was something new, so meeting her meant it was time to move on. When the short overlap of relationships ended, Ritina and I started dating. I loved her ... I guessed. I didn't know what love was supposed to feel like, but I knew that as my twenties wore on, I was at the age when it was supposed to happen to you. My brief grasp of logic suggested that since I left a relationship for her, that must mean something. She was from a nearby farming community called Buttonwillow, she was cute, and she didn't interfere with my drinking at all, so what was there not to love? We stayed together for several years before talking about marriage. There was no rushing into things. I felt like I was doing everything right, unlike my parents.

It all led to one booze-fueled night where the fun turned suddenly into an argument. I don't know if I was afraid of losing her or just wanted to end our argument, but I brought the strife to an end when I asked, "Will you marry me?"

It worked. She said yes.

If my life had a mission in those days, and it most assuredly did not, but if it had some kind of covert, unrealized mission, it was an attempt to actually be and seem *normal*. In high school, I had always been horrified by how abnormal and embarrassing my family was. I'll never forget all the scenes Mom caused with her screaming at Dad or the public humiliation of watching Dad get arrested in front of the house, in the middle of town, or in some seedy drug den somewhere. I had always put up a big front of not caring, but my constant desire was to actually fit in with the rest of the world—not just pretend to fit in, which is what I'd been doing for years.

In the small town I was from, there was a certain way people did things, and dating endlessly with no purpose to life wasn't it. You got your home, your picket fence, your stack of bills, and you did what people do in the good old US of A. I can't say I wanted that life nor that I didn't want it.

I had, by now, confined my partying to the weekends with just a cocktail or two, maybe three, on weeknight evenings, but I had no intention of giving up my weekend partying. I lived for it. Ritina didn't stand in my way in that regard, so she was as a good a wife as I could hope for, I guessed. I didn't care what else happened during the week as long as I got to retreat into my euphoria, my ecstasy of rum-fueled pleasure, two full days a week. I didn't dream of backpacking around the world, writing the great American novel, becoming a millionaire, having a house full of kids, getting a truly fulfilling job ... I was young, thus (technically) full of potential, but I didn't dream at all. All I thought about, in my idle moments, was having my next drink. I don't know what Ritina dreamed of. I never asked.

We told Ritina's mother about our big plans, and to my great surprise, a completely crazy snowball called "wedding planning" started rolling downhill. Sadly, Ritina's father had committed suicide when she was young, but her mother Gloria was recently remarried to a member of an affluent family in the ranching business. With Gloria's blessing on the wedding, and the resources she had, the wedding planning went into full swing. I'll be honest, to the extent that I contributed to the snowball effect of the planning, it had more to do with my excitement over a big party rather than a wedding. The first indications of trouble should have been my proclivity to call our nuptials "the party."

I thought my parents would be pleased that I was getting my life together and building a future with someone, like my sister had done, but neither of them were. Whenever the topic of the impending wedding came up, they both gave grumbling, insincere congratulations. Finally, I asked what was wrong.

"Do you love her?" asked Dad.

Honestly, I had no idea he was such a romantic. My response involved hesitating and shrugging and babbling, so he stopped me. "You should marry someone you love," he said. "Not just do it for the sake of doing it."

Mom agreed. We had the conversation several times, actually, but I didn't know what was meant by love. I thought maybe I did love Ritina. She didn't bother me, anyway. She was all right. We never fought—at least not like Mom and Dad did. I had never had a girlfriend I liked better (or worse) than her, for that matter. So, that was love, wasn't it? My worry was: what if I waited for this mysterious thing called "love" and eventually discovered that what I had with Ritina had been as good as it gets, all along?

Also, I'd met people in love. They argued with each other. They got angry and screamed, then made up and gushed with adoration, which frankly exhausted me. What's more, people in love tried to do everything "as a couple," and it led to endless discussions and conflicts and problem-solving adventures. Their lives were wrapped around their love for one another and the endless work of sustaining and nurturing it. I didn't want all that work and drama. I got my kicks from drinking, not love, and the people I liked the most were those, like Ritina, who didn't stand in the way.

My parents' aversion to the idea of this wedding was probably more than them simply being concerned about my romantic life. In reality, they knew a thing or two about compatibility, believe it or not, and they couldn't see Ritina as any kind of a fit for me. Either way, I didn't consider them qualified to give me lectures about "love." They weren't exactly a sterling example of a loving couple, so I found it strange that they, of all people, were bringing up the subject of romance. Together, Ritina and I were "normal," and that was enough for me.

Now, I had a job, and I'd soon have a wife. We were going to buy a house, raise a kid or two, take them to little league games, and so forth. It had never occurred to me that love was the thing that made my parents act so crazy or that they'd prefer for me to grow up to be *in love* rather than *normal*. The whole thing did plant a seed in my mind, though—it made me wonder what love was. Would it grow between Ritina and me? Would I one day feel it for some other girl? Would I know it when I felt it?

The wedding ended up being in a big event tent set up on a hundred-acre ranch, with an open bar and 380 guests. It was a fabulous affair. After all, I had my hand in planning the "party," and it certainly was one. Soon afterward, Ritina and I bought a house and she got pregnant, exactly as planned. The baby was a boy, we named him Anthony, and life was great. I kept my drinking to the evening hours during the week, but come Friday afternoon, all bets were off. I continued to party like a maniac all weekend, every weekend. Why wouldn't I? This was, obviously, the entire point of life. It didn't occur to me there was anything else *to do*.

The difference now, though, was that I'd go out to bars or the golf course more often than not, rather than having friends over to the house, so that my merry-making wouldn't disturb the baby. I considered that a significant compromise I was making to accommodate the needs of parenting and married life. At work, though, I focused as much as anyone. I was a regular guy. In fact, even when I was drunk in the evenings, I was a pretty regular guy. Well, more fun than "regular," but still, I didn't seem like a maniac. I just felt good. One cocktail and all the pain of my childhood, all the fear I'd experienced, all the doubt I had about being loved … it just vanished.

There were moments when I realized how much I needed those drinks. It wasn't just logic, as in: they made me feel good, therefore I wanted them. No, there was an element of having an inability to resist the temptation of alcohol, too. I didn't drink at work, for instance, but if someone has showed up to work with a fifth of vodka in his pocket and asked, "Want some?" I probably would have had a guzzle despite knowing it could disrupt my livelihood. When alcohol was present, I couldn't resist it.

I remember being in bed with Ritina one night after a hard weekend of partying, and confiding in her. "You know," I said, "I don't know if I can stop this."

My wife said nothing. Surely, she had no idea how serious the situation was. In fairness, neither did I. She was probably wrestling with her own demons and had no room in her head for mine. We weren't big talkers, Ritina and I. We didn't tend to stay up late pouring out our hearts to one another. The idea of doing this, in fact, had never occurred to me before, so when she didn't respond to my confession, I figured I should have probably kept it to myself, anyway. I didn't know sharing deep things about oneself was a part of married life. I didn't even know I could enjoy doing that.

Until I met Liz.

The California Department of Corrections worked its magic. I was head of the accounting department, and Ritina was in budgeting – another department altogether. Liz, meanwhile, worked under me in accounting. Liz and I flirted, we flirted harder, and pretty soon I couldn't get her out of my mind. She made me happy, made me laugh, understood me so much better than my wife. Around her, I felt happy *even when I wasn't drunk*, and that was something new, indeed.

I knew I was going to sleep with Liz. It didn't "just happen." It wasn't "a mistake." The affair was very much on purpose and with knowledge aforethought. I slept with Liz once, after which I realized that:

1. This must be what love feels like, and

2. I was a bad, cheating husband, therefore:

3. Ritina would be better off without me.

When I told Ritina our marriage was over, I did so with a sense of charity. I believed that by leaving her I was doing her a favor. She deserved better than me. Our son was six weeks old.

The premise behind this logic was that my being a cheating husband was something I discovered about myself, not something I made a choice about. Sure, I made the choice to cheat, but being a person who would make that choice, you see, was the thing I felt I couldn't control. In my view, I was an out-of-control bad-choice-maker when it came to Ritina. It hadn't occurred to me that I might also end up being a bad-choice-maker in my budding relationship with Liz. I guess I thought she was going to cure me of that.

Before this, I had thought that following the typical trajectory of people in society would bring me happiness. That's why I married Ritina—because marriage is what people do. Now, however, I realized that "doing what people do" was quite boring. It was much more exciting to fall madly in love. And anyway, people got divorced all the time.

What was the big deal? With this new outlook, I changed my life philosophy quite radically and so quickly that I didn't even notice it had happened.

Philosophy aside, drinking used to provide all the happiness I needed. That's why I thought it didn't matter much whether I "loved" Ritina or not. But, just a year into my marriage, I wanted more. My entire justification for leaving my wife and infant son was the beginning of a phase where I started seeking *happiness*, rather than just *normalcy*. What had satisfied me before was no longer good enough.

It had not in the least occurred to me that ensuring happiness for my family members might actually build my own happiness along with theirs. It also never occurred to me that there was any type of love more intense than that between a man and woman. In fact, if you had told me that at the time, I would have looked at you like you were speaking Swahili. If alcohol had taught me one thing, it was that the search for happiness was an entirely selfish endeavor.

CHAPTER EIGHT

Two Marriages

I had thought Ritina would bring me happiness by not standing in the way of my romance with alcohol, but eventually I wanted excitement, too, and novelty, and adventure … and Liz.

I wasn't the only one cheating. Liz was engaged to be married when we had our affair, and she and her fiancé had recently bought a house together. She broke off the whole years-long romance and all their plans together just for me. We were crazy about each other!

Pretty soon, Ritina and I settled our affairs. We sat down at the kitchen table, hammered out the terms of our divorce, paid a lawyer $300 to sign a piece of paper, and it was over. I don't know how Ritina felt about all this, but I don't recall her screaming and throwing plates. In all honesty, I avoided thinking at all about what others were going through.

I left Ritina, rented an apartment of my own, and Liz moved in. We were so happy there. I felt like it was she and I against the world. We really seemed to be deeply bonded. Liz was a best friend, not just a wife. She was everything to me. We talked about getting married, but she didn't care about doing things in the right order. She wanted a baby! Secretly, I wondered if this sudden desire was caused by jealousy over the fact that Ritina brought my son over for visits on a fairly regular basis. I wondered if Liz wanted to get pregnant in order to nail down our relationship. There's no way of knowing what her motivations and true feelings were, but I didn't really care. If she wanted a baby, I wanted one, too. We were forever. Why not start our family right away? Anthony would make a great big-half-brother. It was going to be great!

Sure enough, Liz was pregnant by the time we got married, about eight months after she moved in.

The wedding was a fun, quicky affair at a Las Vegas wedding chapel. My parents came; hers, too, along with her brother and grandmother. Everyone was on board with this one. Or, at least, they put on the appearance of being supportive. My parents liked Liz. Best of all, nobody said a thing about my having left my previous wife and newly born, infant son. Everyone was just supportive of the new marriage all the way around. In retrospect, I don't know whether this was good or bad for me (or Anthony) but we all hoped this new beginning would be just the thing to make a man of me.

After the wedding, my weekend drinking escalated. Although I continued to confine partying to the weekends, I achieved this by redefining the concept of the weekend itself so that it started on Friday, at any time. And, of course, the middle of Saturday night was still a weekend, so there was no sense in skipping one single moment of my "drinking hours." And Sundays, well those were the hours of last resort. I figured I had to pour as much liquor as possible down my gullet all day and night on Sunday so that I'd be fortified for the week ahead. So, gradually, sleeping was a thing that went out the window.

Somewhere along the line, Liz figured out that I was an alcoholic. She knew it far before I did. She had, in fact, grown up with an alcoholic mother, so she could see the signs. She never said, "Hey, I think you have a drinking problem. Let's do something about it." She never said, "You know, honey, AA isn't just for homeless guys drinking out of paper sacks under highway overpasses. Why don't you give it a try?" Nope.

She just packed up one day and left.

I resented that she had never said any of those things. I felt that as my wife, she should have supported me, helped me get sober, or at least given me a warning. Obviously, she didn't feel the same. I suppose, to be truthful, I must acknowledge maybe she did say some words of warning, but I never heard them. Being a survivor of alcoholism in her immediate family, Liz knew exactly what it was when she saw my behavior up close and personal. And no, she did not feel an obligation to help me get sober. She knew I'd have to hit rock bottom, first, and she, frankly, didn't want to be around for that.

In marrying me, I think she thought she was going forward, escaping her family curse, but soon she must have realized that, like so many children of alcoholics, she had, by marrying me, inadvertently jumped right back into the shark tank. Once Liz realized what she had done, she had to look out for herself, and frankly she couldn't pack her things (including our infant daughter, Emily) fast enough.

Losing Liz devastated me. I had thought that with her, and with having recently turned thirty, I'd finally figured life out. Sure, my parents had been right about Ritina being a bad choice, but with Liz, I thought I had finally married the right woman and settled down for good. But no. And with Liz, there was no sitting at the kitchen table and hammering out a divorce agreement. She hired a cutthroat lawyer, immediately.

At the time, my parents were renting a house back in my hometown of Shafter, so I moved in with them. Lost on me at the time was the irony of my return to the family I had prided myself so much on my quick escape. Back home at Mom and Dad's house, I got to have visitations with Emily and Anthony… whenever my two ex-wives allowed it. Now, I had to face who I had become in the space of the last three years, which was the opposite of the kind of man I'd set out to be. I was growing to be more like my grandfather Martin than anyone else in my family—making babies all over town, never sticking with a woman, having kids to support that I'd probably never actually raise. What's more, I stewed on my anger at the world, and at Liz, for doing this to me. According to my logic, none of my misfortune was deserved.

I couldn't (and still don't) recall purposely saying a cross word to Liz, nor treating her badly, although booze-fueled amnesia may have something to do with that. I do recall that when I became aware the wheels were falling off the marriage, I threw a picture at the wall in anger. As it fell and shattered to pieces, I realized my behavior had crossed a line. Still, I felt really abused in the situation. To me, the two of us had taken vows to help one another in good times and bad, "for better or worse," and she had reneged. The fact that a year or two previously I had reneged on the exact same vows I had made to Ritina didn't really enter my mind during this self-pitying time. I was a victim! In my logic, if my feelings were hurt this badly, in fact if I was actually feeling something, daring to feel, then I must be a victim, mustn't I? Poor me!

One night, I was drowning my sorrows as usual in a Bakersfield bar when who should I run into but Brian, Liz's ex-fiancé, the one she left for me just a few years prior. He was miserable, just drinking himself into a stupor, and he unloaded on me. He looked as if he hadn't slept since the night Liz left him. I knew that look. He was more sad than angry, really, and I definitely felt like he was more upset with Liz than me.

By this point, I'd lost her, too, and felt the same way he did. We commiserated, asking who the hell she thought she was, asking how she could justify breaking both our hearts like this. Anything could have happened in that fateful moment. He and I could have come to blows, blamed one another for our interlocking romantic traumas, but instead we ended up outside the bar, smoking cigarettes together. Considering my divorce from Liz was still pending, and her lawyer was trying to take me for whatever I had, the moment's irony was not lost on me.

Even after my affair with Liz and all that followed it, Ritina, Liz, and I still worked at the Department of Corrections. Eventually, Liz found a job elsewhere, which I was glad of, but boy was it strange running into both of them sometimes in the same day. It had been a whirlwind few years, and now I had two babies, two exes, a bank account that had already been divided in half once, and a pending divorce that was likely to leave me with less than a quarter of my original assets the second time around. So, what did I do? Naturally, I drank.

CHAPTER NINE

My Second Rehab

The whole only-partying-on-weekends thing went out the window with my second divorce. I lost track of the days, in fact, and I'd call in sick to work whenever I was too drunk or hungover to go in. It was nearly impossible to get fired from the Department of Corrections, and even if they'd canned me, I wouldn't have cared. After Liz, I was long past caring about anything.

One weeknight—it was six months after Liz had left me—I was partying at a friend's house, where I crashed on the couch for the night. I'm not even sure I had my own place at this point. That was my life: just wandering and drinking, no routine, no obligation to return home (where was home?), no responsibilities except for seeing my kids once in a while, which was easy enough to do, as they were both babies. I woke up early the next morning and knew I was in no shape to go in to work, so I grabbed a cigarette, a morning cocktail, and my cell phone, and went out on the patio for some air.

I called in sick to work and stood there, enjoying the morning air as the sun rose and a beautiful rosy glow painted the landscape. For those who have been to California's Central Valley, you'd know the kind of morning it was. You can smell agriculture, and the dust from fields skews the colors of the morning skyline. It might have been the contrast between the beauty of the morning and the darkness inside me, I don't know, but I just broke down crying out of nowhere— sobbing like a baby. I didn't know why it was happening. It was almost like my body understood something my mind didn't—I was breaking down physically, emotionally, and spiritually, and I was finally at the point where it just all came out in wordless tears.

What are you doing? I asked myself, suddenly becoming hyper-aware. It was as if I stepped outside myself for a minute and stood on the patio like a ghost and, for once, really looked at the figure of Dennis Farmer: a grown man in his thirties, drinking and smoking and calling in sick to work, first thing in the morning, with no hesitation, still living like a teenager, with two babies to support. I had lost the love of my life because of my drinking, but what was I doing, now? Drinking. Drinking used to solve my problems back when "feeling bad" was the only problem I needed to solve. But now my rum-and-Cokes were only causing problems and not solving anything.

I called my health insurance company and told some stranger on the line that I was drinking too much and couldn't stop. I didn't know if there was any sort of procedure for this or if she'd just laugh in my face and tell me to get my shit together. I had heard of "rehab" (who hasn't?) but didn't really know what it was or who went to those. I certainly didn't think of myself as the "rehab type."

I had to call a few different places, fill out some forms, and generally jump through hoops, but I was still fit for the effort, able to talk and reason and discuss the issue with perfect clarity. After all, it was still morning. Luckily, the State of California provides decent enough healthcare that they were able to help me, and within a day or two, I found myself staying at a rehab clinic in North Hollywood.

This is where I was introduced to the group meetings that typically characterize Alcoholics Anonymous. I sat in a circle with a bunch of other guys who talked about being homeless and beating their wives and losing their jobs and getting arrested. These were bad characters, though, not decent guys like me. The program kept me on board for three or four weeks, but I spent the whole time shaking my head at the hard cases I saw there and realizing I didn't fit in. I wasn't that badly off.

Not drinking for nearly a month was hard, sure, but I was young and my body was resilient. I understood I needed to dry out, so I dragged myself through the days and the meetings and did the program. Never once, though, throughout the entire time I was there, did it ever occur to me that I'd never have another drink. I knew I'd go back to drinking, especially once I saw that I wasn't as bad as the real, tried-and-true alcoholics at rehab. I needed a break from the sauce, though, for sure. In my mind, that was the purpose of rehab. Just a break.

When I got out, I felt great, mostly because I'd learned that real alcoholics were complete losers! As for me, I was gainfully employed with a roof over my head and keeping up with my parental obligations. That was what I thought, anyway. Truth be told, I was living with my parents and broke. However, I wasn't a crazed, raving lunatic like those other guys. To me, that meant a compromise: I'd continue to attend AA meetings but make no actual commitment to stop drinking. I didn't need to. I had control, after all. I just needed to scale things back. The AA meetings, at this point, were kind of my personal equivalent of Dad's habit of ironing his ill-gotten money. They gave a certain impression, made me look put-together on the outside. There wasn't anyone I was trying to impress, though, so it was only myself I was fooling. The "money" I was "ironing" with those AA meetings was more than my alcoholism. It was my life of utter aimlessness and pointlessness lacking in humility, lacking in any sense of a higher power or overarching life mission. For a few months, I maintained life this way—thinking of myself as a regular guy who had just gone through a hard-drinking phase and finally returned to normalcy. To me, the meetings were there to ensure I didn't go overboard with drinking, but I did not at all believe I had the disease of alcoholism.

After a few months' worth of meetings, a funny thing happened. I walked into one and who should I see there but Liz's divorce attorney! I couldn't decide if I should stay or leave, but he had already seen me, so I stayed but kept quiet. We didn't acknowledge each other. Knowing I went to AA could have given him a lot more ammunition to use against me, and he was already wiping the floor with me, legally. I mean, this guy was vicious. Interestingly, though, he never brought it up in court, never used my alcoholism against me. He didn't need to, anyway, as he had me by the balls already. At the end of the day, I really respected his adherence to the confidentiality of the program, especially considering he had absolutely no other scruples when it came to making mincemeat of me in divorce court.

Before long, however, a life of meetings alone wasn't sufficient. It was the longest I'd been without a girlfriend or wife in a while. Right about the time I noticed this, I met a girl we'll call Sue. She was the relative of a friend who had also recently started going to AA, so our mutual acquaintances and mutual addictions to substances really introduced us. Her thing was drugs more than drink, which further convinced me I wasn't as bad as the real addicts. At least I stuck to booze! So, she and I started going to AA meetings together, and pretty soon it was clear we were going to start dating. We decided to spend a weekend together, and I think we both knew what that meant. I had never really dated a woman without drinking. I didn't know how to do it, to tell the truth. What would I say? How would I relax in her presence? The very idea of it seemed impossible.

She and I booked a weekend at a hotel, and when we got there, we went to the restaurant, first thing. Wouldn't you know it, but we skipped dinner in favor of drinks … we both knew it would be this way. Neither of us said a thing about AA or rehab. I knew my own justification for returning to the lifestyle (I wasn't as bad as the real alcoholics!), and I'm sure she had hers. After that, every weekend was a party, again!

Things with Sue and I didn't last more than a few months. We weren't closely bonded, and after a while she found some other guy and took off with him. It was a relief to me, actually. I picked up and left our apartment, which had only been quickly thrown together to resemble a home, anyway. I found myself living at extended-stay motels, mostly. I was still working for the Department of Corrections but calling in sick whenever I wanted. I was right back to the lifestyle I'd been living after Liz.

Then, it happened again.

It was six months after I'd left rehab, and I was having another one of those cocktail-and-a-cigarette sunrise mornings on the balcony of a cheap hotel. A couple of doors up from me, two young women around my age were doing the same thing. From their looks and by listening to their conversation, it was clear they were prostitutes who ran their "business" out of their room. They made no attempt to hide it. One of them bummed a cigarette off me, then returned to her friend, where they smoked and talked together. Listening to them, I almost felt sorry for them.

How did they end up like this? I wondered. It wouldn't be until years later that I'd recount this story and realize I was also smoking and drinking at the same hour of the morning, on the same patio of the same cheap hotel. I had just called in sick to my job, yet again, even though where I was working was only about a mile up the road. I would eventually realize with shame that I was in no position to judge those girls. In fact, I realized, if I were a woman, I might be living just like them, by now. Even though the irony of my judgment had not yet occurred, this whole morning started me thinking about my life, again.

My first time in rehab hadn't done me much good, and now, I was right back to where I started. My life was going nowhere, but more importantly, my emotional and spiritual life was shit. I was never what you'd call happy, anymore. I wasn't dying or suicidal, but I was never fulfilled or excited about life, either. I was just going through the motions of working, eating, sleeping, and drinking. When I got bored of it, I'd move. The little adrenaline hit I got from moving and experiencing someplace new was the closest thing to happiness I could manufacture.

I didn't aspire to own a home or marry again. I visited with my kids, but I wasn't raising them. They were just that: visitors in my life. I had lost all sense of having aspirations. I had given up and succumbed to drink as my only driving force in life. But I just knew I was better than that, had more potential than that. I didn't want to be this guy!

So, a couple of weeks after that morning I spent next to the prostitutes, I returned to the same rehab clinic as before. The people there looked at me with a knowing eye. After all, this is a story as old as time—most addicts take a few trips through rehab before they really "get it." For me, this was only trip number two.

This time, I was in worse shape than before, and they had to put me into a detox program for a few days. This is where you're hooked up to IVs and monitors and given drugs like Ativan and Klonopin to help you manage while they flush the alcohol out of your system without too much pain or withdrawal. It's quite horrible, but not as bad as detoxing on your own, which is the ultimate horror. You've seen it in the movies. Guys tie themselves to their beds and tell people not to let them loose even if they become madmen, screaming and begging for mercy. Detox is a much more civilized, medically supervised version of that.

When you've graduated from just plain "rehab" to the full "detox" experience, you know you've taken things further than before. You've either moved up a level in your drug or alcohol use or you've simply gotten older, and your body won't bounce back like it used to. For me, it was both. This is where I genuinely started to wonder if I was actually as bad as those total degenerates I'd met the first time around.

Men and women are separated in rehab, but detox is a different thing, as there are only about a dozen people in there and it's a bit more casual, not segregated. Folks go out and smoke on the patio in between medications and things, so there's a bit of socializing. That's where I met Erica, who was also detoxing. We had a few chances to play cards and chit chat, and somehow, I knew she was different. We seemed connected in some strange way, and I thought she saw it, too. Yes, I had just left a disaster of a short-lived relationship to return to a life of fulltime drinking. Yes, I was in a detox program. But my urge toward serial monogamy had not been diminished.

This, however, is a trap a lot of folks in rehab fall into. It's called "thirteenth stepping," where the bogus thirteenth step in recovery is falling in love with someone else in recovery. Typically it happens after completing a program, not on day two, but I digress. These relationships seldom work out and often lead to both partners relapsing. Personally, I felt like my feelings for Erica were something different from this, something special and "meant to be," but that's how thirteenth-steppers always feel. By this point, an outside observer probably could have told me that, so far, my idea of what was "meant to be" was far from accurate, but, inexplicably, I still trusted my own instincts.

After detox, Erica and I both went into our separate rehab areas, where we each stayed for a month. Once in a while, we got a chance to wave at each other behind the watchful eyes of the staff, but for the most part, Erica and I didn't speak to each other at all and both concentrated on getting sober. For me, it was getting sober *again*. During this second rehab stint, I was a bit more convinced that I had a real problem, not just a slight lifestyle glitch. But honestly, I wasn't completely sold on the idea that I was an incurable alcoholic. I did, however, take the program seriously enough that when it ended, I went ahead and moved into a men's sober living house right next to the facility.

Sober living is basically dormitory living for recovering alcoholics. It's looser and less monitored than rehab, but you have to get a weekend pass if you want to go away, and there are curfews. Living like that is an admission that you stink at managing your own life and need an authority figure and "house rules" to keep you sober and to keep you straight. If you're ready to accept that you need external structure, this lifestyle can be really helpful. So, I tried it.

I got an AA sponsor this time, too. I was definitely attempting to get clean, and it didn't outwardly show that I still wasn't actually committed to staying sober forever. That was just something I knew, deep inside. I still thought I was just a guy who had overdone it due to some jarring life events—two divorces right in a row!—and I still saw myself as a victim of Liz's cruelty.

I continued to marvel at how she could have left me so suddenly with so little justification. I wondered how our love had gone from true, desperate, and utterly real to something she was willing to just toss away. I felt sorry for myself and, frankly, didn't want to rule out the possibility of ever using alcohol to soothe that feeling, again. In some ways I needed to be a victim. It would allow me an excuse should I need one, again.

CHAPTER TEN

Nothing but a Dirt Clod

"Look who's here!" one of the guys shouted over the din of people chatting on the lawn.

Ice clinked in my soda pop as I jumped up to greet Erica, who had wandered over to one of the barbecues at the men's sober living house. She was bashful around all these guys, but what with our newly sober status, we were harmless. I got her a burger with the fixings the way she liked it and greeted her daughters Leila and Alyssa, who tagged along. There were a few other kids there, who would visit on the weekends from time to time, so the girls being around the house wasn't awkward.

Living here wasn't bad. It wasn't comfortable, either, but it wasn't bad. Kind of like being married to Ritina. I just did it. It was what you were supposed to do. I stayed sober and had plenty of friends to hang out with, but inside, I wasn't committed to this life. I was just trying it out. Despite two stints in rehab and one in detox, I still simply couldn't see myself as someone with the disease of alcoholism. I had always considered myself a basically healthy person with a good head on my shoulders. How could I have a *disease*? I didn't talk about any of this with Erica, though. I suspected, in fact, that she wasn't staying sober. If she were sober, I should think she'd want to talk about it, how hard it was, and stuff like that. She knew I was staying sober, so she'd know we had that in common, but she never brought it up. I didn't care. I still felt like Erica and I had some kind of incredible cosmic connection. That feeling never went away, no matter how many months we spent sharing burgers and sodas at barbecues.

When Erica finished rehab, she had returned home to her girls and apartment in an eight-unit building on Mentone Avenue in Los Angeles. It was the same building where her mom, dad, sisters, aunts, uncles, cousins, and huge extended Syrian/American immigrant family also lived. Her building wasn't far from me, though, making it easier to drop by the barbecues. I think these little weekend get-togethers were the highlight of both of our dreary weeks. We got to know each other better. I really liked her. I wasn't just looking for a woman to fill some empty emotional place in me, like I'd done before. I didn't even think it was a good idea for me to be dating at this stage of my life. Erica wasn't a place-filler like that. She was someone that seemed to actually *get* me.

Erica never came over drunk, but she seemed too relaxed to be on the sober track. It was funny because both of my ex-wives drank, but neither was an alcoholic. Now here was Erica, who knew about detox and rehab and relapsing and alcohol destroying your life and making it all someone else's fault and judging other drinkers and then judging yourself for judging them, and the endless cycle of it all… but others in my past had shared those similarities with me, too, and we hadn't had a strong connection. That's how I knew my thing with Erica wasn't circumstantial. It wasn't about us sharing a similar lifestyle and similar problems but something deeper than that.

After a while of living like this—the barbecues, the group get-togethers—I knew I wanted to date Erica in a more private setting but didn't know how to ask. Somehow, I did ask, though, and she must have said yes, but I have literally no recollection of this phase. I know she somehow agreed to a date, though, because this sent me into an absolute tailspin of anxiety. I really wanted this to go well, and I simply knew that if I was sober, it wouldn't.

Even though I had just got out of rehab, being with Erica at that point felt more important than staying sober. In spite of the incredible pain and discomfort of detox and in spite of the boredom and frustration of the entire rehab experience and all I had gone through and all it had taken me to get there, I still didn't value my sobriety above all else. Deep down, I think I thought that being loved by someone else was more important than respecting and caring for myself. I may too have thought that being loved was the ultimate problem, not the booze. It's a trap a lot of alcoholics fall into, and just like the other dummies, I fell, too.

I thought I was pretty smart, though. After getting a weekend pass from the men's sober living house, I went to a motel room, stocked up on Bacardi Gold and Diet Coke and ice, and sat with the TV on and got drunk. All by myself. It was my preparation for our date the following night. With the three or four months of sobriety I had under my belt, I felt more clear-headed, but not like myself. Clear-headed wasn't *me*. To date Erica, I felt I needed to return to the old charming me, the party guy, mister good-time-Charlie. But would I be able to? Could I still summon him? I needed to practice drinking to see if my old self was still in there, somewhere. I also needed to see what kind of hangover I was going to be in for. By the end of that night, I had the lay of the land of my new drinking-on-special-occasions version of me and felt ready to go.

When I took Erica out, we drank immediately and hooked up the very same night. There was no hesitation, no caution, no conversation about whether or not this was a good idea. I told myself this was because we liked each other so much and had such a special connection, but it was probably just because all we knew how to do was revert to old habits. I continued staying at men's sober living, pretending to be sober, but I'd take weekend passes and get loaded with Erica on a regular basis. It went on like this for a few weeks. Then, in one of our conversations— talks that became more grandiose now that alcohol was involved— she mentioned to me she had never been camping.

I thought that was cute. I mean, I'd been going camping my entire life. It was a fun way to get loaded with friends, not have to drive anywhere afterward, enjoy the warmth of a campfire and the howling of the wind in the trees, and it barely cost anything. Also, when camping, you could stay on the beach, in the mountains, and in places with incredible views where you could never afford to actually live. I made fun of her for being a city girl. Then, of course, I took her camping.

We drove up to the Central Coast of California and chose a campground right on the beach, just the kind of place that felt like luxury. In the morning, you could make your coffee on your little camp stove, then walk out to the water and sit there watching the waves, sipping the warm brew, just soaking in the salt spray, the pink and orange sunsets … I wanted to show her the freedom of it all. So, we pitched a tent and did just that.

"You're right!" she said. "This is pretty nice!"

The entirety of the first day, we enjoyed our usual cocktails.

Naturally, we were surrounded by others at the popular campground, so, throughout the day, we greeted our neighbors, like you do, and we made friends with the couple right next to us. They were very happy and talkative. I wasn't paying much attention to them, but Erica had more of an eye for people. Also, for drugs.

The only drug I had ever tried was marijuana and didn't like it at all. It made me high but mostly just ravenously hungry followed by desperately sleepy. That was exactly the opposite of the life-of-the-party persona alcohol gave me, so weed wasn't my thing. I had consumed weed on occasion, but only as a byproduct of being drunk – and even then, it was rare. Luckily, our camping neighbors did not offer us weed. They offered us cocaine. If memory served, it was Erica who actually asked. To this day, I have no idea the secret code that allowed her to know the camping neighbors even had cocaine.

In for a penny, in for a pound, as they say. So, with Erica's encouragement and after watching her set the example, I tried a line and discovered instantly that cocaine made me somehow able to drink more alcohol and get more of that nice, drunk, jazzed-up feeling I liked. I was an instant fan. Our neighbors were generous. I think they were actually dealers and had a nearly infinite supply of the stuff. As a result, by the second or third day of our camping trip, Erica and I were laughing and talking all day long, having the time of our lives.

One evening, as we walked back from the beach all sandy-haired after being windblown and sundrenched, holding hands, giggling at some little in-joke, she turned to me and said, "You know? I want to get married."

I thought she was joking. She knew my history with marriage. We were both a couple of two-time losers with kids from different spouses, although she had never married the fathers of her two kids. *Then again*, I thought, *shit happens to everyone*. We were both still alive and kicking and trying to find happiness, just like anyone. So, would one more try really cause any harm?

I pulled her aside into a stand of sea grass. Behind Erica, the sun sat above the ocean horizon, like a fat piece of fruit, threatening to touch the horizon but not quite ready to commit. I recalled an old expression of my father's and asked, "If we had nothing left in our lives but a dirt clod … is this what you want?"

Dad used to always say that: "If we had nothing left but a dirt clod, would you…" It was a way of trying to take a choice outside of the context of your real life and make you see it from another angle. Would this thing still be important under completely different circumstances?

Erica looked at me with total confidence and said, "Yes! I do! I want to get married!"

We talked about it for about one minute, then I shrugged as one does at so many of life's inevitable milestones. It seemed to be just another grandiose alcoholic idea, though. I didn't know if it would ever actually happen.

"You want to get married? We'll get married, then!" I said. That was that.

We continued along the path back to the campground, laughing and giggling together, feeling more in love than ever. When we passed our neighbors/friends/cocaine dealers, they asked what we were laughing about.

"This one wants to get married!" I blurted out.

"That's great!" the lady said. "You should have a barefoot, beach wedding!"

"Great idea!" I said. Then I opened my mouth and proceeded to do that thing we alcoholics like to do—continue making grandiose plans with exciting details and outrageous embellishments. I went off about what a grand wedding it would be, one day, but the lady interrupted me.

"No," she said. "I mean it. I have a friend that's a minister. She can be here in an hour."

I pulled Erica aside and asked if she was really serious.

At the thought of getting married immediately, Erica lit up, even more overcome with joy than before. Her smile stretched from ear to ear as she nodded and affirmed, "Yes! Yes! I really want to!"

So, it was only about an hour and a half later that we stood on Pismo Beach, still in our bathing suits, alongside our camping neighbors whose names I don't remember (or perhaps never even knew), who were our witnesses, and a minister said words over us.

The orb of the sun had committed, finally, to its descent into the ocean while distant clouds showed silver linings and elegant purple streaks, and I looked at my third wife with all the glee that cocaine and Bacardi Gold and true love could send coursing through my veins. Her eyes were starry, too, as we kissed to seal the deal. Our witnesses, whoever they were, applauded and whistled.

The next two years were absolute hell.

CHAPTER ELEVEN

Nothing Good Happens on Mentone

I followed the minister's instructions by driving to City Hall for a marriage license the Monday after she married us and bringing it back to be signed by her. This necessitated Erica and me staying one more night at the campground, which cemented the fact that I had entirely disregarded even the pretense of following the rules of my sober living house. My "weekend pass" had turned into a drunken, drug-and-drink-fueled, four-day extravaganza. It was just as well that I planned to move in with Erica, because they didn't need influences like me in a place of recovery.

I moved my few boxes of stuff into Erica's not-at-all-sober apartment, only to discover that her Middle Eastern mother and grandmother, Mexican father, sister, uncles, aunts, and cousins had no boundaries whatsoever. Any of them would just walk into our home at any point, day or night, and take what they wanted, talk about whatever they wanted, complain at length about any old thing. There was no locking of doors and absolutely no limit to what they felt they had a right to know and say and do in Erica's life. Meanwhile, none of them had any idea who I was or where I came from and showed no interest in finding out. I was interested in them, though, as their family history was pretty dramatic.

Erica's mother's side is from Bethlehem, the notoriously embattled holy city in the West Bank. Ceded to the Palestinian Authority in 1995, it was occupied by Israel before that, and Palestine again before that, and Jordan once upon a time. It had been Jordanian when Erica's mother was born there, so she considered herself from Jordan. It all seemed very discombobulating, but they were used to it, and anyway, they were all Americans, now. These women had brought the chaos and strife of their homeland with them across the continents and oceans of the planet, sadly making no attempt to find peace, either inner or outer, along the way. Erica's father, born in Mexico, was also proud to be an American, now. As the only male presence around, he might have provided a strong and grounding influence, but no. Instead, he was content to remain locked away in his corner of his apartment and let the women go at each other. We didn't tell them we were married. It just seemed like one more thing that would bring on her relatives' incessant criticism, insults, and endless generalized harassment.

To say these people were unhappy would be like saying the Titanic sprang a little bit of a leak, one day. They thrived on unhappiness. They were, in fact, only happy if they were *un*happy and busily telling the world about it. Having something to complain about was the goal of each of their lives. At least, that was true for many of them. Later, I gained a bit of sympathy for them when I learned the depths and sources of some of their unhappiness and how very complicated it all was.

Then there was my wife's ex-boyfriend, the father of her four-year-old daughter Alyssa— a deadbeat of a human being if I ever saw one. Just your friendly neighborhood drug dealer, this guy had been given his walking papers by Erica about a year and a half previous but couldn't seem to accept that it was over. He came over, uninvited, on a daily basis. I don't mean he showed up at the door with a bashful look, a toy for his daughter, and flowers for Erica, I mean he screamed from the sidewalk up through our window at midnight, demanding that his toddler be awakened and shown to him in the middle of the night.

Some of the chaos around Mentone Avenue was cultural, and I didn't understand it. But the chaos related to Erica's ex-boyfriend was different. For one, he was white, so he had no cultural excuse. Second, he was just a bad human being, one with whom I had no patience. In an attempt to quell the chaos on Mentone Avenue, I started making rules about who could visit when, and what constituted a middle-of-the-night emergency.

Of course, my rules were laughed at and so was I. So much for starting off on a good foot. The situation was made worse yet by the fact that Erica is the opposite of a fun drunk. When she drinks, "belligerent" is a kind word to describe her.

Erica, who is about a buck twenty soaking wet, will fight anyone and everyone, challenge the world, and take insane risks when drunk. Sober, she's actually quite shy and introspective, takes her time to warm up to people, keeps a tidy kitchen, and ensures the children do their homework with stern kindness. I never saw sober Erica in that apartment building, though. I just saw the screaming banshee. But I loved that screaming banshee. Whatever drew us together was a strong force. Back then, I didn't have a name for it, but I knew it was real and much deeper even than what I thought I'd had with Liz.

Despite her alcoholism and crazy home life, Erica had managed to keep a job as a branch manager at Wells Fargo for many years, just by adhering to the strict code of having two separate lives. Unfortunately, this troublesome drug-dealer ex was threatening that security by making it his fulltime job to cause problems for her, mainly because of me. That said, it's pretty hard for a single man with a juvenile manslaughter conviction (whose only means of support involves a case filled with pills in the trunk of his car) to gain custody of a child, but this joker would be damned if he didn't try. I think it's safe to say it wasn't so much that he loved his daughter but rather that he wanted to hurt Erica for having tossed him out on his ear.

He kept coming by, taking his daughter away for a while, bringing her back, yelling at Erica about any old thing, and later screaming through the window in the night. He never stopped. The way she and I were drinking at this point, there was no point in calling the cops, as they wouldn't know who in the building to arrest. They might just go for us all. Erica's nine-year-old, Leila, was luckier in that her father didn't seem to thrive on drama. Stories would occasionally emerge about past drama when he'd been in the picture, but those days were over. By the time I entered the picture, he had long since moved on with another woman.

When I went into rehab that second time, I took a leave of absence from my job with the Department of Corrections, and when I married Erica, I was still on leave. Ever since, I had been living very cheaply on my savings, or on unemployment, but by this point, I needed to figure out something for stability. I couldn't handle returning to work for the state, knowing both my exes worked there and just knowing how dreary and depressing correctional institution work could be. So, I pounded the pavement during my few sober-ish hours of the day until I landed a job as an HR manager for a plastic surgeon in Beverly Hills.

Pretty soon, I was back to the old lifestyle of work during the day, cocktails at night, and weekend binges, except that this time I had to watch out for Erica, who could really get herself into legal and physical trouble when she drank, due to her overwhelming, irrepressible hostility to all authority, real or imagined. Taking care of her centered me. I liked it. This was the first time I ever felt responsible for another person, especially one so vulnerable. I had two children and two ex-wives, so this doesn't make sense, I know, but that's just how I felt. I also liked how taking care of Erica kept me from thinking about myself (and feeling sorry for myself) all the time. I still drank, though—naturally, we both did.

I had been to rehab twice by now, and I'm ashamed to say that (besides Erica) nothing in my life was better as a consequence. In fact, everything was worse. Despite how much I loved her, living with Erica gave me a whole host of problems I had never had before. With the chaos of her home life to deal with, neither of us really thought quitting drinking would solve any of the problems. Where she lived, it was nothing but a hive of bees, just buzzing, buzzing, buzzing to beat the band until you couldn't hear yourself think. We had to do something to take the edge off. Even so, I felt like for the sake of sanity, we really had to take the girls out of that building and move far away. I had thought my own upbringing was chaotic, but it was downright peaceful compared to what my stepdaughters were living through. I felt for them but was utterly trapped in that unquiet environment, just as they were.

Trying to get to know my stepdaughters in the midst of this madness was an impossible task. They just tolerated me, and, as a "family," we kept on trying … just withstanding, withstanding, withstanding the madness, day after day, keeping our marriage a secret until the day that I somehow won over the hearts of her family members with … I don't know… magic?

They all probably figured I was a fly-by-night boyfriend of no consequence. Under the circumstances, they couldn't really be blamed, but I didn't intend to be. In spite of all our troubles, my original feeling of being bound to Erica, being destined for her, had not changed one bit.

CHAPTER TWELVE

Arrested

One night, I opened our bedroom window to smoke a cigarette. The bedroom was on the second floor of the apartment. I had a little ashtray I kept on the outside window ledge, there, so I wouldn't have to walk all the way downstairs and outside to smoke. Of course, I had a cocktail in hand as well. That evening had actually been a good night, for us. Alyssa had her cousin staying over, and they were playing peacefully. Leila was at her dad's, and Erica and I cranked up the music and danced in the living room. We got nasty looks from my sister-in-law as she passed the window, but that was par for the course. All said, it had been a good night.

Strangely, as I leaned my head out the window to smoke, an LAPD officer standing in the building's driveway immediately shone his flashlight in my face and screamed at me to open the door. It came from out of nowhere. I wasn't even sure he was yelling at me, at first.

As it didn't look like I had much choice, I stubbed out the cigarette, returned inside, and sauntered towards the front door, but the officers, now plural, didn't wait for me. By the time I reached the living room, they had kicked in the door and were screaming at me to get on the floor.

I did exactly as I was told, which didn't seem to make them any happier. Then, Erica emerged from the bedroom, drunk and screaming, "What are you doing in my house?" and so forth.

Two officers cuffed me, picked me up, and hauled me outside and into the back of a police cruiser. Meanwhile, Erica's deadbeat ex stood conspicuously across the street, filming the torrid event on his phone and screaming, "How's it feel now, bitch!" I wasn't sure if the bitch in question was me or Erica. Despite having a good buzz on, I did realize the timing of him being present for this event couldn't have been a coincidence.

Naturally, Erica escalated her (understandable) objection to this strange and violent break-in and kidnapping until they had to also haul her, literally kicking and screaming, down the stairs and into the back of a different car.

It wouldn't be until later, at the police station, that we were told a neighbor had called that night and reported seeing a woman being strangled in our apartment. I could see that our loud music might have annoyed a neighbor or two, but there was no way some bad dancing could have been mistaken for strangulation.

"What are you talking about?" was all I could say. Then, I remembered the deadbeat.

Erica and I both spent the night in jail, which really made no sense at all, especially in Erica's case. *If she'd been the victim of domestic violence, why was she arrested?* I wondered. Later, I found out that, out of eye-shot from my back-seat vantage point, Erica's verbal assault against the officers turned into her kicking out the rear window of the squad car she'd been thrown into. She shrugged and I chuckled when she later recounted that she had "needed air."

With my one allotted phone call, I had managed to get word to my Dad. Who else would I call? So, the next day, when Erica, of course, did not file a complaint or press charges against me, Dad, with money from Uncle Bill, would bail me out. Promptly, I made freeing Erica our next priority, and by the end of the night, we were home.

I'd never been in trouble with the police in my life. My father's example had been enough to keep me on the straight and narrow where criminal activity was concerned, so this was highly irregular. We attended the court date, which was a group situation like traffic court, where you sat in the court room and the judge called up the different defendants while they each waited their turn. Finally, lunch break came around and we still hadn't been called. The judge asked why we were there, so we gave him our case number, and he said he didn't have that case on his docket. From here, we had to go and see some other guy. We jumped through hoops like this for a while.

Eventually, we found ourselves sitting across from a city attorney who told us no charges had actually been filed against us. In front of him was a file that, presumptively, held our information, but he refused to show it. He went out of his way to describe our entanglement with law enforcement as a "detainment," not an arrest. At first, it was a ton of bricks removed from our shoulders – we were free! Then, we got mad. What the hell had happened, after all? Why on earth would a neighbor call about a woman being strangled? Had they come to the wrong apartment? What was this all about?

We would eventually hire an attorney, although hiring is a deceptive word when the law firm is willing to take a case for free. That's more common than you might think when you want to sue the Los Angeles Police Department. Ultimately, the case would settle with no real vindication other than the fact that it didn't cost us, or our free attorneys, anything. We did, however, find some answers about what happened.

The concerned citizen neighbor, the one who saw "a woman being strangled," turned out to be friends with the deadbeat ex, himself. The only possible conclusion we could draw was that the two of them had conspired to present her as a concerned neighbor calling the cops about a domestic violence situation. The point of this whole charade was to get his daughter Alyssa taken away from Erica so the tyrant would get custody, which is exactly what happened.

We fought to get custody back, which involved a lot more filling of forms and standing in front of judges. It seemed like we'd inevitably win, but we couldn't convince Erica's family members that the whole thing had been a hoax. They wanted to believe the worst about me, so they went ahead and did, despite all evidence to the contrary. It was all terribly depressing and demoralizing, but we kept fighting.

Then, a man came to the door one day with a manila envelope. He thrust it at Erica and told her, "You've been served!"

Turns out, Leila's father was also filing for custody!

Erica showed up drunk to her court date for that one, and that's all she wrote. She lost both of her kids within a couple of weeks. We had been married less than six months.

I worried that I'd been the cause of all this. The domestic abuse allegation wasn't true in the least, but if I hadn't been there, the thug couldn't have made up that particular story. And if that hadn't happened, the other father probably wouldn't have filed for custody, either. Erica showing up drunk to court … well, that's just what alcoholics do: tie one on at the most inopportune time. Even though she loved her daughters, it's the kind of thing she would have done in any case. Then again, if I hadn't been there, who knows what physical violence that deadbeat would have attempted against Erica, living alone with her daughters. So, surely, my presence in the family hadn't been all bad. If he'd tried anything, it certainly wouldn't be the first time he'd laid hands on her. No, the snowball might not have rolled downhill in precisely this way in my absence, but I wasn't the cause of her problems by a long shot.

In any case, Erica and I weren't going to be torn apart—not by her family members, her exes, the legal system, or anyone else. Unlike in all of our previous cumulative relationships, we both still wanted this to work. Naturally, being alcoholics, our primarily allegiances were to drink, not each other, but each other ran a close second.

CHAPTER THIRTEEN

Homeless on the Beach

Without the obligation to give my stepdaughters a semblance of a normal life, and with this new level of hostility from everyone around us, Erica and I finally locked our doors, refused to pick up the phone, and isolated ourselves. The house was quiet without the girls in it. All we could hear was the clinking of the ice in our glasses.

Every time we left the house, it seemed like a million people were peering at us through covert slits in their Venetian blinds, so we would rush to get into our car and speed away. It was a stressful existence, almost like being under house arrest. Many outings happened in the cover of darkness. We began walking to the liquor store instead of driving out of sheer terror we'd be confronted by someone. Walking gave us more flexibility in case we needed to run or hide.

Erica usually returned from work after me, so it was strange when, one day, I got home and there she was, having a drink at the kitchen table. "I quit," she said.

She'd had her job at Wells Fargo for ten years. Now, all she felt fit to do was sit home and drink. She was officially falling apart, and fast.

I made it another week before I quit my job, too. I couldn't leave Erica alone all day like that. She was, inevitably, going to go out and get herself arrested for one thing or another if I wasn't there to stop it. So, we stayed home, and we drank, and that was that. She had nothing going on in terms of problem solving. She had lost her kids. Her world was a zero, and she didn't care about living. I got that. But rent was coming due. I was going to have to figure out a solution.

We remained in isolation for a month, at least. Meanwhile, we sold what little we owned and packed the remainder hastily into boxes. Then, as a last resort, I called Dad. To my amazement, there weren't any words of judgement, and in short order he arrived with a truck to move us. We were leaving Mentone Avenue, finally, although we were more battered and bruised by our time there than either of us could have ever predicted. Once more, I found myself living with my parents. Once more, the irony of returning to them in such a state of desperation escaped me.

We stayed at Mom and Dad's for a few months— an excruciating length of time, as the depth and severity of my drinking were on full display. Privacy of any kind was a thing of the past. There was no hiding it, no isolating, and we knew we needed to get out of there. While we tried to figure out an escape plan, Erica and I would seek moments of privacy by disappearing for a few nights here and there when we could, camping out in the car, or getting a seedy motel room— anywhere we could escape and drink to our hearts' content.

I was still on a leave of absence from the Department of Corrections. It didn't pay to quit the State of California once you were in the system. So, although I hadn't planned to work there again, I'd never actually burned my bridges. I made some phone calls and ended up getting myself a job helping activate a new prison being erected out in California City, in the middle of the Mojave Desert. The middle of nowhere.

The job was easy to get, as few people wanted to live in that hellscape of a no-man's land, so they sweetened the deal by ensuring I'd be getting paid well in a place where everything was dirt cheap. I could support my wife while she worked to try to get her kids back somehow … or not. I didn't know what she wanted to do, and neither did she. There was still a chance she'd go out drunk during the day and get into trouble, but at least we'd be making a clean start away from her family members, her thug ex, that evil neighbor in league with him, and everyone who thought I was a wife-choker.

At first, it was a relief to get an apartment in no-where's-ville. Being away from Erica's suspicious relatives was, for me, like having a fresh, clean breeze blow through our lives for the first time since our weekend on the beach. I almost couldn't believe I was through with them. For my wife, there might have been a part of her that missed them. They were her family, after all, but she never said so. The main thing was that she missed her girls so much she couldn't really talk about it, and she was deeply depressed. I knew it was my job to help her ... but how?

The result of my failure in this regard was that I upped my alcohol consumption to match hers. Now, it was cocktails in the morning, a pick-me-up at lunch time, and then ... it was hard to make it through the rest of the work day without another drink, but I usually succeeded. I poured another cocktail as soon as I got home, though, and things escalated from there, every single night. When I stopped off at the grocery store, it was never for milk and eggs but just Bacardi Gold and Diet Coke. Our grocery bags didn't rustle. They clinked. We ate less and less until we were barely eating at all. Why bother?

I lasted six months in that job, and then I just couldn't, anymore. Physically, emotionally, spiritually, I just couldn't work. Especially physically. It was almost like I had booze coursing through my veins instead of blood, but it needed to be constantly topped up, like the oil in a leaky engine. Without a few capfuls of booze for energy in the morning, I was like a wind-up toy without the key. I couldn't pay attention, either, to anything, except getting loaded. Anyway, California City was a hideous, ugly place, and once I stopped going in to work, we had no reason to be there, anymore. So, we left Mojave.

It was at this point that I truly felt lost, especially since a return to Mentone Avenue was the only option. I dreaded the idea with every fiber of my being, but we did it and wound up staying with the very relatives I had come to despise. They hated me, after all, so, I figured, why should I have any sympathy for them? Nonetheless, they allowed us to stay and even provided us with our own room.

It was during this time that I heard that music—the most incredible classic rock-and-roll songs of all time. The tunes seemed to just bleed right through the walls, as if all the apartments around us were having simultaneous house parties with identical music. Remarkably, I knew all the words, even to songs I had only a vague memory of. My ability to recall lyrics seemed to be exceptional! In retrospect, it's clear that such a thing would have been highly unlikely, but, at the time, I believed the music came from the neighbors. After all, I'd never had a hallucination before. This was all new territory. I never thought a hallucination would sound like that—like the music was literally coming from outside me. But then, when the music was replaced by demonic voices, Erica called an ambulance.

At the emergency room, they gave me something for the hallucinations but told me it wasn't a cure for alcoholism. The doctor there warned me if I didn't start drinking water and eating food and wean myself off the sauce, I wasn't going to live long. Looking into his tired eyes, I saw that he had met a thousand Dennis Farmers already in his life, and I was not special to him. I was just another bombed out loser at the emergency room. His sadness for me shamed me. I had never envisioned myself as someone people would view with pity or despair, but here I was. And here Erica was, and this was what our lives so far had come to. I could see the epitaph on my grave already: "Here lies another bombed out loser. Nobody special." It was depressing, so, naturally, I cured my depression about being an alcoholic with my panacea: more alcohol!

At this point, neither of us could handle living another day on Mentone. There was only one place Erica and I had ever really been happy together: Pismo Beach. So, we returned to the scene of the crime, grabbed a campsite, this time on the actual beach, and just hid from the world. We had no money, anymore. Somehow, we managed to scrape together enough for a bottle of booze now and then, to keep us going, and we'd ration it out as much as possible. That was more important than food or water, for us.

Various other campers would show up, and we'd make friends with them, pretending that we had just arrived a few hours before. We pretended to be the people we'd been a year or so ago—just an innocent-ish couple in love, out for a fun weekend, seeing the sights of the beautiful

Central Coast. We'd make friends with the folks passing through, saying we planned to head home in a few days. Then, just when they were leaving, when we were supposed to be leaving, too, we'd always laugh and say we had decided to stay just one more night, for kicks! Nobody suspected we lived in our tent, full time.

We had no future plans, no ideas for making money, no hope of ever finding a home, again. We had no wants or desires and, frankly, I think, deep down, didn't plan to live long, although we never talked about that.

Alcoholics Anonymous was a distant memory and the importance of the program had entirely faded from our view. All we wanted to do now was drink. Quitting wasn't really possible, as our stomachs were destroyed. Food wasn't an option. Our meager rations of booze were probably all that was keeping us alive. I was down to about 140 pounds— fifty pounds underweight for a six-foot guy like me. Erica tottered around on spindly legs. We lived like that for twenty-eight days.

Even in the midst of all this despair, though, the wheels were still turning in my head. If it hadn't been for Erica, I don't think I would have been motivated to problem-solve at all, but I wanted to help her more than myself. She had been dealt a terrible blow and, yes, she had made it worse by showing up drunk in court, and, yes, there might not be any coming back from that, but I was a drunk, too, so I sympathized.

Although I had no resources to speak of, I wanted to help her survive, make her happy again. If it had been just me on that beach, I would have died. I wouldn't have given a damn. But having Erica to take care of pushed me on. What I did next was a shot in the dark, just a random idea for a guy completely out of ideas. I called my old high school buddy Brad Wiedmann.

Naturally, I didn't tell him what a bad state I was in, I just acted like I was reconnecting, saying hello. He was glad to talk to me, though, so, as the call wore on, I admitted that, due to a variety of circumstances "out of our control," my wife and I were a bit down on our luck. I told him about her ex, the deadbeat, and what he'd done but didn't include a lot of other key elements to the story. Brad was sympathetic, and as it turned out, he had formed a house-flipping business in L.A. with his brother-in-law Steve. He told me he owned an empty home Erica and I could stay in. In fact, we'd be doing him a favor by keeping an eye on it. This was such an unbelievable offer—a life-saving offer, really—that I worked to keep my breathing steady while I wrote down the address he gave me. We were going to have a home, again! Without any nosy neighbors! And it was free!

When I told Erica, we didn't waste a single minute but took down the tent, packed the car, and bid a somewhat sad farewell to our beloved Pismo Beach, with its beautiful views, gentle surf, warm campfires, and cocaine-fueled wedding memories.

CHAPTER **FOURTEEN**

I Can Drink More than You

The house Brad lent us was definitely a fixer-upper but a real mansion compared to homelessness. It had electricity and running water and everything, so Erica and I took advantage of the situation by bringing our things inside and then running out to spend our meager funds on booze, to celebrate.

At this point, I made the big decision to switch from Rum and Coke to vodka, because it didn't smell as strongly. I was hoping this would mask the fact that alcohol was basically seeping out of my pores. I'm sure the switch did nothing of the kind, but it made sense to me, at the time. Consider the clarity and purity of vodka! The lack of sweet aftertaste! It was practically a health food! And it was cheap.

Erica and I were actively dying from total malnutrition and alcohol poisoning, but finding this place to live had been such a coup that we literally couldn't think past the phenomenon of having a roof over our heads. On the way to Los Angeles, our car finally broke down. Ironically, the only reason we still had it was because the finance company couldn't find it. By the time we arrived at our new home, the trip itself had taken everything out of us. After all, the only thing that gave us energy to keep living was alcohol, the very thing that was also destroying us, and the one thing you couldn't use for energy on a long drive. I was aware, at this point, that I had to watch out for driving drunk, but I never really knew if I was, technically, drunk. Maybe I was past the legal limit all day every day, or maybe I never was because I assimilated alcohol so fast, now. I had no sober gauge by which to measure drunkenness. This was one of the reasons I knew we needed to stop living out of our car. But now, it didn't matter. We were walking.

We stayed in that house for a few months or so, and then Brad and Steve got ready to renovate the property. The whole time, we had no gainful employment or hope of ever having jobs, again. Erica's depression over losing her kids put her in a state where she couldn't imagine a future, so I just took care of her, kept her alive, kept her safe. That alone was such an effort, day to day, that there was no time or energy left for thinking about what we were going to do when we ran entirely out of money.

During this time, Brad and I used to go out drinking in bars, just like the old days. He simply thought (because it's what I told him) that I had fallen on hard times due to circumstances beyond my control and was amazed that he could actually drink me under the table, now! Unlike in my youth, I definitely showed signs of being drunk by the time I'd had a few cocktails. He didn't know I was an alcoholic slowly digging my own grave. He just thought I'd been on some kind of amazing weight loss plan and was proud of himself for being able to match me drink-for-drink, now. Meanwhile, I was glad and kind-of amazed that Brad still enjoyed my friendship. It was the sum total of what I had to offer, after all.

Brad was such a good friend and put so much effort into trying to help me, I almost couldn't believe it. I didn't feel worth his effort, that's for sure. In fact, I knew I didn't deserve this outpouring of love and resources he was giving me, but Brad and I—born on the same day in the same year—were bonded from birth. He was like a brother to me. He didn't have to be, though. A lot of time had passed since high school, after all. Brad wasn't helping me out of any sense of obligation or pity, though. He didn't even know how down and out I really was. He's just a nice, caring person who helped me out of love. I'll never forget it.

Brad finally came up with an even better idea for Erica and me. He and Steve owned a down-and-out, seven-unit apartment building in Bakersfield. It was a shithole of a building in a shithole part of town, with five shitty people living in it, only two of whom ever bothered to pay their rent. Erica and I could live in one of the apartments in exchange for collecting the rent from the tenants. The presence of "management," Brad hoped, might pressure the tenants in arrears to settle up. If we managed to improve the revenue at this place, we'd even get a small stipend from it—enough to keep stocked up on cheap vodka, anyway. We said yes!

Once we moved into Bakersfield, the little bit of an income we got did nothing to straighten us out. Quite the opposite, in fact. Now that we "had it made," Erica and I indulged in the luxury of total, worry-free alcoholism. Now, I never had to get behind the wheel of a car, at all. Two liquor stores were right across the street, along with a school and a church. It was a horrible part of town in which to be out walking on the street, but I guess we were now an integral part of what made this part of town so horrible to begin with, so we embraced our fate.

Erica and I drank so much in Bakersfield that we became intensely paranoid. I wouldn't drive, of course, which was a realistic form of paranoia, but I also wouldn't go into the bedroom. I was scared of that room, so we slept in the living room. I can't say what I thought was going to happen in the bedroom. The fear had no basis in reality. It was just a delusion. This useless and repetitive existence was, itself, exhausting.

Then, one day, a Wednesday, after a trip to the liquor store, I had nothing else to do, and, to be honest, another one of those voices was giving me ideas. So, I wandered over to the little church across the street. They had a sign out front announcing when services were, so I read it and noticed they had Wednesday night services at six o'clock. I wandered home after that, poured myself a stiff one, and kept drinking until six o'clock. Erica wasn't interested in leaving the apartment, but she never asked why I was putting on my good shirt and going out to church. I don't remember if I opened up my wallet and ironed my money before leaving, but I might have. I hadn't done that in years. That's what my dad would have done, though. He would have wanted to place crisp, perfect bills in the offering basket, to show he was a man of class. He wasn't, of course (at least, not in the days I remember him ironing money) and neither was I, but those crisp bills, for him, were more than just a way to pretend to be someone he wasn't. They were a way to cling to a tiny vestige of hope. If one thing about him was nice, perfect, straightened-out, and crisp, then maybe more of him could one day be that way, as well. So, whether I did it overtly that day or just in my mind, that impromptu church visit was my way of ironing what was left of the currency of my life. I was trying.

At the church, everyone was welcoming and friendly. Nobody wrinkled their nose at how I stank or looked down at me. Considering this part of town was chock full of drug addicts and degenerates, I was surprised and delighted to find a whole bunch of nice, sober, and very pleasant people, there. They reminded me of the folks Brad and I grew up with. Straight-forward, small-town folks who cared about their neighbors just because they were neighbors, not because they'd "worked hard" or "earned it" or anything like that. They cared … just because.

I didn't have any kind of overwhelming epiphany that night, I just really liked the welcoming atmosphere. For a very long time, I hadn't felt like I deserved friends and pleasantries and welcoming words from anyone, yet here were these complete strangers willing to invite me into their little world. It was nice.

CHAPTER FIFTEEN

My Third Rehab

When I puked, it came out as a yellow or green bile. The vodka was clear, so that didn't affect the color of my vomit, and anyway, I never threw up alcohol. What a waste that would have been! No, I only threw up when I tried to eat. After that church service, I wasn't enlightened or anything, but I did have a little bit of a feeling that I might try to take care of myself better, so I tried eating, but to no avail.

Prior to this, I had thought of food as something I couldn't afford or wasn't in the mood for. I had always assumed I could start eating again, anytime I wanted. But now, I realized I was dying. And Erica, she too was dying, probably faster than me. All the security Brad had given us out of the kindness of his heart had only encouraged us to kill ourselves faster. By continuing to not take care of ourselves, we were shitting on Brad's wonderful gift, thumbing our noses at the one person who cared about keeping us alive. My parents, at this point, began to extend unexpected kindness towards us. My Dad worked at the property, and Mom would show her concern by visiting, but we didn't want to hear what they had to say and rebuffed them.

It was around that time that I looked at myself in a full-length mirror for the first time in a long time. What I saw was horrifying. I'm normally a regular sized, broad-shouldered man, but all I saw in the glass was a scarecrow, a skeleton. A skeleton can't take care of a wife. A skeleton has no use in modern America ... except as a skid-row cautionary tale. It wasn't one big epiphany but a lot of little realizations over the course of a few weeks (including the one church service I had attended) that led to me deciding to get sober for a third time. Even that statement is probably a stretch. I don't know that I was necessarily trying to get sober, but I was trying to get help. It wasn't so much that I wanted to live as that I wanted to do something other than *this* with whatever was left of my life. I wasn't suicidal. I don't know if the same could be said about Erica. Either way, though, I didn't care if I lived or died, just didn't want to go down like this.

Erica laughed when she watched me, with a cocktail in one hand and a phone in the other, calling around to detox facilities while making my situation worse by the minute. Admittedly, it was a pretty ridiculous situation, but at least I was making the calls. That's when I told her exactly what she didn't want to hear: "If we're going to make it together, it's going to have to be sober."

I would no longer commit slow suicide with her. I was done. She laughed some more, refusing to take me seriously. After all, I was no longer associated with the State of California, had finally let my long-standing relationship with the Department of Corrections go by the wayside, so I was trying for a miracle. At this point, me saying I was going into rehab was like saying I was going to start a colony on Mars, and she could come along if she wanted. Just utterly ridiculous!

"It's happening, Erica," I told her. "And if you want to keep drinking," I said, "go ahead. Have a good life. We're done."

Even though I hadn't found a rehab center to take me, yet, I called Erica's mother, who hated my guts and still thought I was a strangler. I asked her to come pick up Erica and take her "home." I said I'd retrieve my wife after my detox, if I survived, and if she still wanted to be with me, and if she could try to get sober with me. I had no idea if Erica would want me afterward or not—or if either of us would survive the next month or so.

Shortly after I made the call to Erica's mom, I reached a hospital in Long Beach that agreed to take me in with no insurance. It was detox, not rehab, but it was a start.

Her mother wasted no time in getting there, and when she arrived, she barely spoke a word to me as she gathered Erica and her things into the car. It wasn't a pretty site. Erica didn't want to go and seemed to think I was abandoning her. I didn't think of it that way, but I wasn't entirely sure she was wrong, either. I just knew I was definitely going to die if I didn't seek some kind of help, which Erica either didn't want or wasn't ready for. I knew it like I know the sky is blue. I packed up Erica's things, put her in the car, and fastened the seatbelt over her lap, saying everything was going to be okay. She was too weak to fight her way free and looked at me as if I'd betrayed her deeply, permanently, and there was no coming back from this.

Interestingly, during the time it took me to drop to rock bottom for a third time, my father had started cleaning up his act. I had been in touch with him and Mom quite a bit since I moved to Bakersfield. So, even though I was afraid and ashamed of what I'd become, I called Mom and Dad, confessed my lifestyle, and asked them to drive me to the hospital.

Naturally, I got as loaded as was humanly possible before my parents arrived. This would, I figured, be my last time, my last drink. In fact, when it came right down to it, I now regretted having done all this work to get into detox and nearly cried at what I'd done to myself. When Mom and Dad showed up at the apartment building and saw the condition I was in, the looks in their eyes said it all.

They hadn't exactly raised me in the lap of luxury, but we'd tried our best to be as respectable as possible under our circumstances. When your mother is barely sixteen years older than you, and your father comes from a history of abandonment and abuse, and your only set of grandparents is estranged, your version of respectable is going to be a far cry from everyone else's. But still, they tried. And I had ended up here, looking like skin and bones, having abandoned two children and two wives so far.

They had tried to give me a better life than this. They really had, and with my sister, they'd succeeded. She turned out okay, but not me. I felt ashamed of what I'd done to myself, but not too ashamed to ask for help. I guess, in a way, knowing Mom had forgiven Dad time and time again, stayed with him through his infidelities, bailed him out of jail, and even defended him against me—it all made me realize there was nothing I could do, either, that would make her stop loving me. Dad was the same. He was always going to be there for me. I knew that not because he'd always been there for me in the past—he hadn't been. I knew it because our family had always been there for him while he struggled to grow up while also raising two kids. We hadn't abandoned him even when he abandoned us, time and time again. Now that Dad was more stable, he was sticking to that ethos. We might be a family of misfits, but we were a family, none-the-less. That's what their presence meant to me, in that moment, when they drove up.

I don't remember if I tried to back out at the last minute or not. I think I was too drunk and weak to get many steps away, anyway. Dad basically grabbed me by the scruff of the neck and stuffed me into the car. I don't remember the details about getting to the detox hospital. I only remember that once we got there, when we were out in the parking lot, I was either unwilling or unable to make the trip from the car to the building. Dad had to go inside and recruit a security guard. Together, they muscled me out of the car like a sack of potatoes and dragged me through the doors. He did what needed to be done and didn't add anything about being ashamed of me. Didn't add anything about my being a disappointment. My parents were remarkably supportive under the circumstances, maybe more so than "perfect" parents would have been. After all, they were no strangers to rock bottom. They'd seen their own versions of it and survived, themselves. Essentially, they believed in me.

The experience of detox was much like it had been the time before, but this time was longer, and I didn't have Erica's smiling face to take the edge off for me. I slept through much of it, and the IV drugs feeding into my system helped. I lay there for three days, barely conscious, just letting the fluids and benzodiazepines do their work.

After three days, my parents called, and I still wasn't coherent enough to talk to them. I was grateful they cared enough to make the call, though. Someone still cared about me. I couldn't believe it! In the meantime, nurses had informed them that even on the third day of detox, I still had some blood-alcohol content. I also had pancreatitis and a swollen liver. I was skin and bones. Basically, the hospital had nothing to report to my folks on the phone except my continued status in the land of the living.

I lay bedridden for yet another week, but after those first three days I was **more** conscious and able to talk to the hospital staff. I told them I was grateful for the detox, but I knew I was going to go home and drink again. As sure as God made little green apples, I was going to drink again. I didn't know how to live any other way, didn't know how to be happy any other way. Even as the booze drained out of my system, I was dreaming of my next cocktail. I had already been to rehab, had already been to Alcoholics Anonymous, had a wife and two children and two step-children who needed me, and none of that helped keep me sober. I pleaded with the doctors and nurses for an answer while never really believing one existed.

The days wore on, and I knew that as soon as my system was clean of booze, as soon as I was rehydrated, they'd tell me to go live my life … "and don't let the doorknob hit your ass on the way out."

I begged everyone I saw for something else, something to save me from myself. What that would look like, I did not know, I just knew I feared being on my own. I was my own worst enemy. Basically, I needed a bodyguard to protect me from myself.

"I don't know what to do!" I pleaded. "I'm going to go home and drink again! I don't know what to do!" It was pathetic to listen to myself, but I really couldn't think of anything else to do but plead. I was little more than an animal in a trap, at this point, ready to chew its own leg off to survive.

One of these nurses took pity on me and, on her own time, made some calls to I-don't-know-who. She came to my bedside on the next to last day of detox and said she knew somebody who could get me a scholarship bed at a residential rehab in Anaheim. She was like an angel. I don't know her name. I've tried to find it out, since then, but I never have been able to.

My parents called again on day nine, and I was able to tell them the good news. Someone who knew how to take care of me was going to do so. How, I didn't know. Why, I didn't know. All I knew was that I wasn't going back to Bakersfield to drink myself to death. At least, not yet.

My parents picked me up from detox and drove me down to Anaheim, not letting me have a moment to myself in-between. They did not stop for gas or snacks or anything where I might be able to get loose and find a drink. Ironically, after all the time I'd spent with the Department of Corrections, my parents took me to rehab like a couple of expert prison guards, which was exactly what I needed.

The next sixty-days would change my life. For the first thirty days, though, there was still some fight in me. I still wasn't sure if I intended, or needed, a life of complete sobriety after this. Having been detoxified, I felt so much better than I had in months, perhaps years, that a part of me thought I was, "all better, now!" The insanity of that thinking is quite remarkable to me, now.

I remember arriving at the facility. It was right around dinner time, so they took me upstairs to put my stuff down and show me my room. I emptied my pockets out on the nightstand—gum wrappers, lint, a few coins. Then, I went down to the cafeteria to eat. I actually ate!

When I came back upstairs again, though, I sensed something was different. Then, I saw it. On the nightstand, where there had been nothing of significance before, sat a Celebrate Recovery Bible with a post-it note on it that said, "To the next guy."

This is a type of Christian Bible with all the usual text in it, but with some pages added in just for twelve-steppers. It's meant to help addicts see how the Bible's principles and the teachings of Jesus directly relate to recovery and abstinence. I'd seen these books at other rehabs but never really sat down and read one. Aside from that one church service I'd attended in Bakersfield, religion had never been my thing, never something significant in my life. Sure, I'd been forced to go to church as a child, but it never really took. Calling me "a believer" would have been a joke. Interestingly, this wasn't a Christian rehab, just a secular one, so surely nobody associated with management had put the Bible there. To this day, I don't know who did it.

With nothing else to do, I sat down that very evening and read. I was thinking how funny Brad would find this—the guy that used to drink him under the table every weekend was now spending his evenings reading the Bible, of all things. I was thinking how Erica would have laughed in that way that indicated an absurdity had occurred, a way that meant, *The Bible? Seriously? Who are you and what have you done with Dennis Farmer?*

And yet, I kept reading.

CHAPTER SIXTEEN
A Bible and a Notebook

Most of the other guys in rehab spent the last unscheduled hour of our evenings playing dominoes or shooting hoops. Rehab tends to offer wholesome entertainment in abundance for those who want to relax during their time away. It's all good distraction, but, for once, I didn't want distraction. By this point, there was no question in my mind that rehab was where I belonged, and if I wanted to live, this experience needed to change me, for life. I no longer considered myself better than anyone else in there. I no longer looked at others who had robbed convenience stores or stabbed people and said, "He's worse than me! I must be okay!" No. That attitude was finally history. This time, I was as pliant as a newborn calf and did whatever they told me. I did not rebel, either in my actions or in my deepest heart. I submitted. It was here that the memory of the prostitutes returned, and shame overcame me as I recalled the way I'd judged them.

So, while the others entertained themselves during the last, unscheduled hours of each evening, I sat on my bed and read the Bible I'd been gifted. If I'm honest, I didn't understand a lot of what I read. I could tell there were surface meanings to the Bible stories and subtler, metaphorical meanings, too, but my brain wasn't exactly functioning at high capacity. I just kept reading and hoped something of value would absorb through my skull.

Maybe it was the Bible and maybe it was simply the time spent alone in silence, but I finally realized that I had no sense of my own soul, my purpose to life, or that life had any meaning at all beyond the endless search for momentary pleasure. Here in rehab, there was, technically, no "pleasure" at all, so this fact came into bold relief. Sitting there with the Bible, I couldn't even experience the adrenaline rush of winning a game of checkers or the endorphin rush of dribbling a basketball and shooting hoops. I just existed, recovering from an even worse existence. I didn't know why I still wanted to live. Just to continue existing? To put in the effort to stay alive after this, I'd need a reason, a direction, and I didn't have one. It had never before occurred to me that such a thing as a higher calling existed. I didn't know what else was out there but hoped there was something. So, I kept reading.

I think I came from a long line of people (at least on Dad's side) who had no sense of life's purpose, at all. Dad had been a petty criminal but with a vague sense of importance around his role as a father. Following his example, I'd say I, too, had accomplished becoming an itinerant father figure to two kids. Four, if I include my step kids. Mission achieved. Was that all there was to life? I was ashamed of thinking this, but being a father didn't do that much for me, at least not yet. If it was meaningful, wouldn't it have kept me off the sauce? Well, it hadn't.

Dad's own father had been an even higher-level criminal who just drifted through life until he was splattered across a freeway. I saw no purpose, there. Then there was my great grandfather Farmer. He had been a preacher, so he must have had a meaningful sense of life's purpose, but I never got to know him. His religious zeal certainly hadn't transferred over to many of the subsequent generations, so I never saw that sense of purpose in action or adopted it, myself.

I had seen, as a child, my mother's hard work to support Janee and me paired with my parents' constant fighting, financial troubles, and the soured relationship with Mom's parents. Keeping the family together against all these odds seemed to have been my mom's driving life purpose, and I respected that ... but what had really been the point? While growing up, my life had been so topsy turvy that I gained independence at an early age, just to get away.

Sure, when I'd married Ritina I had thought that, like my parents, we'd stay together against all odds but soon realized we wouldn't be happy. So, what was the point of staying together? I didn't want to follow Mom and Dad's topsy-turvy model. Janee had followed that model, though—marrying, staying together, having a family, and letting that be life's purpose. With Erica, I thought I had finally latched onto that desire to stay together with someone, too, and made it my purpose to life, but "being together" hadn't been enough for us. And the obligation to support a family hadn't been enough, either. I realized that I had fallen into the booze because I needed a higher calling even than that.

I contemplated these ideas for thirty days, just attending my counseling sessions and AA meetings and reading that Bible every night, trying like hell to pick up some kind of meaning from it, not sure if it was taking or not. During the second month of rehab, my brain seemed to return to me. I was having what could be considered coherent thoughts tied to life plans tied to a sense of what you might even call "meaning." I began to look at my resources. I had a wife that loved me but was at home boozing it up, even as I sat in rehab. She might even have gotten herself arrested by now. Who knows? I asked myself what else I had—well, I had my friend Brad and his generosity in allowing us to live at the apartment building. Him giving us that place to live, along with a chance to earn a meager living, had been a Godsend. Not a lot of people in my position still have friends as good as Brad. Thinking about that made the wheels start to turn.

I hadn't gone to college and didn't know math or business or academics or computers or biology or really much of anything, but I did know what it was to be an alcoholic. Any other education I'd received had been on-the-job or real-world experience. This being my third time through rehab (fifth if you count the two detox episodes), I guess you could call me an expert. I deeply understood the arrogance of thinking I wasn't as bad as the "real" alcoholics. I understood the denial behind thinking of rehab as "just a break." I understood the total surrender necessary in order to say, "My name is Dennis Farmer, and I'm an alcoholic" and know the truth of it. I understood what it was like to live in a men's sober living house and go out every weekend and get wasted anyway—the guilt about bringing my own bad influence to the others who were trying so hard. I also understood the urge to relate to women, to want companionship, sex, children, relationships, and yet to feel that I, alone and sober, wasn't good enough for any woman.

Having been to rehab so many times, and having found various creative ways to pay or avoid payment, I had actually gained a keen understanding of the economy of rehab, too. By this point, I understood that, to insurance companies, we alcoholics represented a certain expenditure every few days we were in a facility. Thus, they always tried to find ways to get us "graduated" so we would stop costing them money. The harder they tried to save money, though, the more people relapsed and died. This, I realized, was a big part of the tragedy of addiction.

I understood the economy of sober living houses, too. In places like that, it was to the residents' advantage to not have their own rooms or ever be alone. It was to their advantage to live in dormitory conditions under strict rules, paying per bed, much like a monastic order. I also understood that this system, while cheap for the residents, brought in more income per room than it would have otherwise. As a matter of fact, a sober living house, when done right, was actually a pretty viable economic model. All you needed was some alcoholics determined to get better, some beds, and an apartment building. Among my meager resources, I had access to all of those.

I had never thought of myself as an entrepreneur, before. I'd never even fantasized about running my own business, with all the sweat and toil that would entail. Before everything fell apart, I used to like working for the Department of Corrections and the way I just had to go to work, be a warm body, do my job, take every possible opportunity to goof off, and then go home at the end of the day and not think about it for a second. But that lifestyle had only contributed to my sense of meaninglessness about life. Imprisoning people certainly didn't give me any sense of a higher calling. I didn't enjoy seeing men humiliated and caged. It was just part of the system I worked for. I realized it would be bad for me, psychologically, to go back to spending my days in that environment. Anyway, for the first time ever, I actually had a better idea.

The reason I'd been afraid to leave detox a few weeks before and was still afraid to leave rehab was that on the outside, I simply didn't have anything of value to do other than drink. So, I found a notebook and pen and started jotting down ideas about turning the Bakersfield apartment building into a men's sober living facility. It seemed like a can't-lose proposition. It would help Brad make more money off that crappy building without doing any expensive renovation. The place just needed to be freshened up with minor repairs and painting, and I'd need to purchase some additional beds, which I could get second-hand, and I'd rearrange things so that there was a central gathering area, but that wouldn't be hard. Put in a wall. Take out a wall. I had seen these things done, before.

I knew from experience that alcoholics who couldn't hack it on their own (like me) and needed to live in supervised conditions were not exactly picky. We were used to being down and out. Many of us had been homeless before and considered an affordable roof, four walls, and a bed to be luxury living. What people like us needed, more than anything, was someone to both enforce the rules and actually give a shit about us, even when we didn't feel we deserved it.

I knew that when they finally released me from rehab, I couldn't go back to living in the apartment building where Erica's family was anchored. Those people could drive a saint to drink, never mind a guy like me. I also couldn't go back to living with Erica like we'd been doing, in Bakersfield. We'd just revert to our old ways. At the same time, I certainly didn't want to inflict myself on any more women, especially when dating equated with drinking, for me. I still loved Erica but knew I needed to go into a men's sober living facility if I wanted to live … and this time, *not* cheat. I now understood that the choice of where to live after rehab was a life and death decision—nothing to be taken lightly. I absolutely would never ever again experience the incredible charity that miraculously got me into the last rehab facility on scholarship. Getting that opportunity, with no insurance, had been a miracle that saved my life, and I knew that, like a lightning strike, it wouldn't happen twice.

While at rehab, I talked to Erica on the phone frequently. It didn't look good for us. She was drunk almost every night, making no attempt to clean herself up. She came to visit me, too, and might have been temporarily sober for the trip, but I had no high hopes of us staying together. I wanted to live. That's all I knew. She was now living with her family in that nest of gossip and accusations and family squabbles, but I was definitely going back to Bakersfield, probably on my own. This time, though, I had an idea that felt— dare I say it?— "meaningful."

CHAPTER SEVENTEEN

Sober Living

To his credit, Brad knew nothing about alcoholism or recovery or sober living. He wasn't that kind of a drinker and had never had to experience such things, but he did know business, real estate, and the rental market. When I showed him my notebook full of plans, explained what it was like to be in recovery, and acquainted him with this population of people who actually wanted to live as if in a permanent college dorm, he was interested.

I explained that one room with six beds, charging $200 per bed, would bring in $800 a month. That's affordable for the residents who are trying to rebuild their lives; meanwhile, with just one room, Brad would make more than he'd normally get for the entire apartment. Sure, there were always those who dropped out of sobriety and couldn't make their rent, disappeared into the underworld, and caused a loss for the landlord, but that was already happening with Brad's tenants in Bakersfield. Anyone who lived in our part of town was a potential candidate for that. But people who were actually at least *trying* to get sober and get their lives on track … those were the best kind of tenants to have in a neighborhood like this.

Brad was interested in that and also in the fact that the men in sober living want to be there. Typically, they aren't just living in a rooming house out of desperation, but by design. For alcoholics, sober living houses provide camaraderie with others who share their unique affliction. They provide friends to those who might otherwise not make any. It's a structured lifestyle and a community that prioritizes staying on the straight and narrow. Living in a sober house keeps alcoholics away from the influences of normal society, where a glass of wine with dinner is quite ordinary; a cocktail after work is expected; a beer while watching a football game is the stuff of an enjoyable life. For us alcoholics, those little things, which most people think nothing of, are the first step on the road to hell. Sober living houses keep us away from those "ordinary" aspects of what is daily life for most folks.

Brad really liked my idea and the notion of getting this population into his property, especially with me running the place, because I understood that world so well (by now). His buy-in on my idea was a huge relief to me, because if he hadn't said yes, I'd have to go live in a sober house somewhere else and get a job and try to be that guy, again. This way, I wouldn't just be living in a sober house, I'd be running it, which would, I hoped, give my life a sense of direction, purpose, and importance that nothing else had provided, yet.

They don't really recommend for anyone who's only sixty days sober to get involved in a huge entrepreneurial endeavor like this. You're supposed to keep your life low key and stay away from risk of any kind. But at my last sober house, that advice led me to drinking with Erica, so I was going to run with this idea, no matter what. Brad kept me on my stipend of about $600 per week, and I was content to spend out of that budget to get my venture off the ground on a shoestring.

First thing I did was evict the current tenants. They weren't exactly thrilled, but a lot of them hadn't paid rent in quite a while, so it didn't come as a huge surprise. Then, I discovered the Habitat for Humanity ReStore. Habitat is an agency that builds homes for those in need, and its ReStore is basically a thrift shop for building supplies. Construction companies that overbought supplies like doors, cabinets, lumber, appliances and such donate them to the ReStore, where they're resold at a fraction of the price. The construction outfit gets a receipt for a tax-deductible donation, and everybody wins. I picked up cans of paint, new carpet, bathroom tile, and all kinds of things there, for pennies. So, with those resources and my own sweat equity, I set about transforming the apartment building. It was exciting!

To my great surprise, Dad was all in on the venture. He showed up, possibly to oversee my newfound sobriety, and seemed to be inspired by what I was doing. Dad wasn't an alcoholic himself, necessarily, but he needed rehabilitation from the entire life he'd lived in the past— the hiding, the lying, the abandonment, the manipulation. He saw me changing, and I dare say he took to the example and started changing, himself. It's funny how they say when people have kids young, they and their kids grow up together. I'd say that was true in many ways with my parents.

Dad started changing for the better when he first became a grandparent. With Anthony's birth, I had definitely seen Dad try harder. But his life's improvement really took off, I think, when Dad saw me finally grow up, and he took it up a gear, too. We bought supplies together, painted rooms together, built walls together, and worked the twelve steps together, even though he might not have been aware he was doing it. As it turned out, my recovery was the inspiration Dad needed for the second part of his own life. What more validation could any son ask for?

Ten days into the project, Erica showed up, and I was delighted to see she was sober. To this day, I don't know how she got sober or how she detoxed all by herself. She tells me she barely remembers it. She understood from our phone conversations over the past sixty days that I was deadly serious about getting sober and running a sober-living house. While I was in rehab, she had taken her time thinking about these changes—not taking it seriously at first but gradually warming up to it—and by the time I was out on my own recognizance, Erica had bought all the way in.

If I was going to be a new man, she was going to be a new woman, and that was that. Erica showed up on my doorstep and declared our marriage far from over. We were going to move forward and do it together. A smile spread across my face like a sunbeam. I felt like I'd won the lottery! She had no income, of course, so this now meant two people living on the same $600 per week, but her presence also meant twice as much sweat equity, so the renovations would get done quicker and we'd have paying residents sooner … as long as there wasn't any backsliding.

I had gone into rehab on April 10th and got out June 10th. By August 15th, I had formed an LLC for the facility. Doing the paperwork cost me $800 I did not have, but I saved it up by setting aside dribs and drabs from our weekly allowance. Where there's a will, there's a way. I was now a business owner, and, with Brad's help, had secured my first lease.

With the rooms freshly painted and utilities brought up to code, I became a regular customer at the local Goodwill and Salvation Army stores, where I bought up every twin bed that came in until I had twenty-four of them in six different units. Meanwhile, Erica and I, the "supers," lived in the building's front unit.

This new endeavor barreled forward so incredibly fast and was so quickly successful beyond my wildest dreams that I feel I should pause here to note the incredible gratitude I was already feeling. I still had that twelve-step Bible, and I was reading as regularly as I had in rehab. I felt its presence in my life. Brad's eagerness to try my idea, Erica's determination to get on board, too, the way renovation materials had come so easily, Dad's involvement and hard work, the way sober clients had showed up at the door with their first week's payment in hand … It had all gone more smoothly than probably anything else in my life ever had. I couldn't help but wonder why.

At the Department of Corrections, I had done as little as possible to get by and been barely tolerated as an employee. At my brief job as an HR manager for a plastic surgeon, I had smiled my way through my pain, eventually quitting out of sheer inability to show up. As a homeless person, I had watched my body wither away while I became resigned to my helplessness. Basically, I wasn't used to things going my way. So, why was everything suddenly falling into place? The Bible on my nightstand beckoned, so I returned to reading it, looking for answers.

As usual, I didn't understand much of what I was reading, but I read anyway. I stayed focused on those pages instead of my pain, my exhaustion, my cravings, my haunting memories, my guilt, my shame, my regrets … instead of all the static in my head. I started to wonder if perhaps the secret wasn't any particular message on any particular page, but just the act of my reading the Bible regularly that was making a difference in my life.

That incredible, sudden success and the overwhelming feeling of gratitude that came with it was where my relationship with God began to bloom in my heart. I just could not possibly believe that all this good fortune had fallen on me out of the blue sky for nothing. Sure, I wasn't drinking anymore, so that had a lot to do with my newfound happiness and success, but it didn't explain Brad's willingness to support my plan (which entailed a lot of risk, for him) or Erica returning to me and somehow getting sober, as if by magic. It didn't explain Dad's unexpected support and interest in helping. My sobriety also didn't explain all the energy and inspiration I was experiencing about being an entrepreneur. The sense I had now that my life had direction and meaning had to be due to more than just sobriety.

After all, this had been my third rehab. Three. The first two simply had not left me with any feeling remotely like this. What was different? The fact that I was at death's door when I entered this particular rehab had definitely been a factor. This one had been the rock-bottomiest of all my rock-bottoms, so far. But I felt like it had to be more than that. I felt, now, like there was a spark in me that hadn't been there before—something that can only be described as spiritual.

This time, I finally felt that sense of meaning I'd been looking for. I also felt like I'd been appointed to fulfill a certain destiny. In fact, I almost felt like the decision to start the men's sober living hadn't been my own. Everything about this endeavor fell into place so easily that it felt like I'd been wandering around on the first floor of my life, trying to figure out how to get to the next higher level, and then I stepped on an escalator I didn't even know was there and it whisked me up. Once I was on the escalator, all I had to do was go with the flow.

In truth, I did a lot of work to get the facility up and running, but it didn't feel like work. It felt like inevitability. I was used to having maybe twenty percent of my decisions turn out okay-ish, but now, all of a sudden, fully 90% of my decisions were turning out great and leading to more decisions that also turned out great. It was nice. It was weird. It was, I decided, grace.

With some trepidation, I returned to that little church across the street and started attending on a regular basis. Erica joined me. She told me she also sensed the grace in what we were doing and also had limited ability to put this strange feeling into words. She didn't know what was going on, either, but she couldn't deny that she was somehow staying sober despite having catapulted herself into sobriety on a whim—something that doesn't usually work for alcoholics.

In short order, Erica would feel inspired enough to file for visitation of her girls. Soon afterwards, she got visitation and then partial custody of her daughters. She hadn't really been sober long enough for courts to take her seriously, but they did, anyway. She instilled that trust in the judges. Her thug ex-boyfriend wasn't bothering her at her new home but instead brought the same darkness he'd brought in L.A. through the court system, now, and he was relentless. Not one or two but dozens of court hearings lay ahead of us, including a full-blown custody trial, but she and I persevered through them all. I also worked to restart visitation with my own kids.

Elizabeth had remarried by this point and was happy. She turned out to be pretty easy to get along with, and I started spending time with Emily, who seemed pretty well-adjusted for a three-year-old kid. But Ritina was a different story. As I was a few years sober, now, she begrudgingly allowed me to visit with Anthony, who was five, without much hesitation, but she had since married a correctional officer, and this guy was bad news—angry and grouchy and never pleasant. I did my best to be there for Anthony. We saw each other every other weekend. It wasn't too frequent, but I didn't want to promise a level of commitment I wouldn't be able to consistently deliver. I made a schedule with him that I knew I could keep, and I kept it.

Pretty soon, Erica and I found ourselves waking up to sunshine, going about our business, making friends at church, enjoying the taste of food, having friendly relationships with the sober-living residents, and accepting grateful payments from them. At the end of the day, we'd go to bed and, strangely, nothing bad had happened all day. The next day, we'd wake up and do it again. I was waiting for the other shoe to drop. When was something terrible going to happen? But it didn't. We just kept going. Doing good work. Making people happy. Taking care of our children. Loving each other. And still … nothing bad happened. Finally, after a few months of this, we got used to it.

CHAPTER EIGHTEEN

The Obsession is Lifted

Istarted the LLC in Mid-August, had residents by the first of September, and everything went so well that by December, I decided to branch out and turn this place into an honest-to-God rehab facility, not just a sober house. Part of me was on fire just to stay as busy as possible so I wouldn't think about drinking, and part of me felt I needed to get fully immersed in the world of sobriety, just to stay straight, but a third part of me was honestly on fire to do something meaningful with my life and make up for lost time.

So, I told Brad about my idea for expansion and explained what was needed for rehab. I really had no idea how to run a rehab, though. God knows I'd experienced them from the client's point of view plenty of times, but I was clueless about licensing, hiring counselors, dealing with the medical side of things, and everything like that. What I was doing was kind of like someone who knows how to shop for groceries deciding that qualified them to go and open their own grocery store.

For some reason, though, Brad believed in me. Again, it was nothing short of grace. I wasn't the sort of person who should inspire this level of trust in anyone, but I did. Not only did Brad okay the idea of changing the apartment building into rehab, but he asked me for financial projections, which I guesstimated with a confidence I had no reason to claim. Then, he loaned me money to do it. Grace was all this was. None of this made any sense, and none of it should have been happening.

Our apartment complex included a one-story building with three apartments and a two-story building next to it with four apartments. So, I kept the men's sober living facility in the four-unit building. That's where my income came from. Meanwhile, I gutted the one-story building, tore out a lot of the interior walls, and recreated it with a group room, kitchen, dining room, and offices. Dad had the honor of knocking down the first wall. Erica and I were also living there, in what would eventually become an office, so we got used to breathing in plaster dust and tripping over two-by-fours. We didn't mind. It was exciting. We were quick to realize, however, that a new place would soon be necessary. After all, we had hoped our kids would be back with us soon– at least her daughters. Living at the facility wasn't going to work for that, but this was a quality problem to have.

Best of all, we were busy every day—too busy to drink. We were also in a race against the loan Brad had given us, trying to turn a profit before we had to ask for more money. Once upon a time, Erica and I had nothing to do all day but sit on the sand, watch sunsets, and feel the life force draining out of us. Now, it was work, work, work and deadlines, deadlines, deadlines. We were alive, again. Or, perhaps, alive for the first time. Dad's involvement become more substantial, too. He was a regular fixture at the apartment building, tearing down more walls, pulling up carpet, and laying down new floor covering.

Whenever I had to do something I'd never done before and really had no clue about, I'd pray on it. Sure, I'd google it, too, and see what others had done, but there isn't any rule book for how to start a rehab on a budget. It just isn't something most people do. Rehab clinics are typically run by corporate conglomerates. They build relationships with insurance companies that pay just enough to push addicts like me through the system and send them packing as quickly as possible. The money they pay per client dwindles the longer the addict stays in rehab. This yields a limited per-client profit for the corporation, so the key to success is *turnover*.

That system, by the way, usually works exactly the way it did for me—clients relapse and return, relapse and return. Because of how insurance payouts work, rehab clinics make more money on clients that relapse and return than on those who stay longer and actually go into lifelong recovery. In short, they are not rewarded for success.

Naturally, I didn't want that. I dreamed of creating a rehab that actually worked the first time. How? I didn't know. That's why I prayed. I sought God's guidance for everything from finding a misplaced hammer to filling out licensure paperwork. Somehow, I always got it.

I had some friends from my most recent rehab who knew a bit about the agencies that did accreditation and licensure. On the strength of their advice, alone, I bumbled through the legal aspects of the business. Somehow, in time, everything got done. Those guys also helped me design the facility's day-to-day functioning. I remember sitting at my desk until three in the morning, just typing out operational procedures and creating an employee manual and thinking through every aspect of how we'd work with clients. This was the part I think I was good at. I had a strong vision for ways to work with clients better than what I had gone through during my own rehabs. I knew the pitfalls, such as thinking "I'm not a real alcoholic" because so many others were worse off and thinking rehab was just "a break" from the drinking you know you will return to. I wanted to help clients avoid going down those roads and slowing their progress.

I also wanted to bring joy to people. I know how alcohol, or any addiction, can zap the joy right out of your life. You live to drink, and you drink to live, and the idea of actually being happy seems like something for another class of people. With this in mind, I'd sometimes do spontaneous things with the clients, like once I took them on a camping trip. We had a full house of eighteen, and I packed them all into our two vans and took them to a local beach, where we pitched tents and roasted marshmallows over a campfire. It was a lark and also a way for people to let down their guard, get to know each other and build community. Sitting around the campfire, we all shared stories about our lives and troubles that simply would never come out in the formality of an AA meeting. For me, much of the inspiration to recover came from the knowledge that a community cared about me (starting with that little church across the street). I wanted to build that sense of community, not just put people through therapies and meetings.

Luckily, all this work served to keep me sober. It gave me a sense of purpose I hadn't experienced, before. The endless work of building the facility and applying for the treatment license simply didn't give me enough time to drink, and before long, I realized I had been sober for eleven busy, exhilarating months and four short days.

At that point, I joined Brad on a business trip to South Carolina. I thought it would be nice to get away for a couple of days. There, we met up with friends of his and went out to dinner, where they ordered a bottle of booze for the table. I sat there talking about Brad's properties and whatnot, trying not to seem overly fixated on the bottle; meanwhile, my fists were clenched under the table. I didn't even realize it for a long time, then, when I finally saw what I was doing, I realized I really really really wanted a drink. After all, I was doing great. I was a regular paragon of recovery. One drink wouldn't hurt me, would it? I was still thinking like a normal person, not an addict. I started thinking I could enjoy every-thing in moderation. But addicts don't do moderation. We just don't. That's the crux of our problem, not just with alcohol but everything.

Finally, unclenching my fists under the table, I asked Brad, "Hey, pour me a drink, why don't you?"

He picked up the bottle, approached my glass, and turned to me, asking only, "Are you sure?" He wasn't going to babysit me, after all.

That one question was all it took. I paused. A voice in my head said, "No! No! No! No!" and then I said it out loud. I didn't want the drink, after all. For the next hour and a half of that dinner, I sat there fake-smil-ing and white-knuckling it, fists clenched under the table. Every minute or so, my desire for a drink resurfaced. I pushed it down. Again. Again. Again. Interestingly, I have never had an urge or compulsion to drink again, after that. Somehow, that night, the desire was purged from my system. The obsession to drink was lifted. It has never returned.

Finally, the rehab license came through. Since the men's sober living facility was profitable, Brad leased one of his properties to my growing company, and I moved the guys there, opening that building up for the residential part of the new rehab facility, which I called Legacy Village.

Technically, I opened the residential facility in 2016, but then I was faced with the question of how to get clients. I had avoided ever mentioning to Brad, or anyone, that I had no idea how to fill beds once the clinic was set up. No one asked. I guess I assumed it would somehow just *happen*. After all, there are a lot of alcoholics out there. Don't rehab facilities just automatically fill up? The answer to that is a definitive no. This is where I faced my next hurdle, and it was a real learning experience.

I couldn't afford to hire a doctor to be on site full time, so I contracted with someone in the community. That doctor, in turn, introduced me to a man who called himself a rehab marketer. It cost twelve thousand dollars to hire this guy, but he swore he could bring in clients with paying insurance policies. I borrowed more money from Brad and Steve and everyone who would lend me a dime, and—with great reluctance—paid the guy. Twelve thousand dollars, then, was a fortune to me, but it seemed like this was the priming of the pump my new facility needed.

Sure enough, the rehab marketer immediately found me a woman and two men, all alcoholics with good insurance policies that had low deductibles and high reimbursement rates. Supposedly, these three hailed from different locations, but after they moved in, it became clear they already knew each other. That was kind of strange, to me.

Soon, we also discovered the female client was pregnant. This wasn't all too uncommon in rehab, so we looked into providing her with the necessary medical care. I went above and beyond to make sure we could get her access to everything she'd need over the next couple of months, even though these services were outside of our system. But then, quite strangely, after eleven days in the facility, all three of them left, "ACA," meaning "against clinical advice." One minute they were residing in their respective rooms, and the next minute, they were nowhere to be found. Gone without a trace. I didn't know what to make of this. First, it was horribly disheartening. We had really gone to great lengths with our meager resources to provide care. Despite the advice against it, we put heart into the treatment we provided, and the clients' sudden worried the entire team. Second, it meant their insurance would stop paying, but since it takes months to get insurance payments, anyway, we hadn't actually received a dime for treating them thus far, and now I had no idea if I'd ever get paid.

That happened on a Friday. On the following Monday morning, I received a call from my medical biller. She was a specialist who did billing for quite a few facilities. "Aren't these three people clients of yours?" she asked, and recited their names. I answered yes but told her they had all mysteriously left ACA. "Well," she told me, "they just got admitted to another facility that happens to also use me for their billing. Their names are now on a different company's roster."

It didn't take long for me to learn the scam. The rehab marketer had offered these three the opportunity to check into my facility, telling them to stay a while, then he'd pay them a thousand bucks or so to leave and go out and get loaded for a weekend. Then, he recycled all three of them by checking them into another facility that had paid his $12,000 marketing fee. After all, the marketer only promised to get me insured clients, not that they would stay until they were well.

This was the beginning of my education in the dark underbelly of this business. Not long before this, insurance companies actually used to pay generously for rehab and have incredibly lax oversight of such facilities. So, clinics overcharged like crazy. For instance, they'd bill $1200 for a urine test and do urine tests twice a day. Basically, many rehab facilities were running scams on insurance companies. The tables turned when insurance carriers realized what was going on. They responded by tightened up on everything having to do with rehab to the point where the scam was now going the other direction.

Now, clients are lucky to get more than six days in a rehab facility with basic, bare-bones treatment. Six days is nothing. The notion that any alcoholic can recover in six days is beyond ridiculous, but after those six days, insurance companies require the facilities to apply for extra days, give specific reasons, provide treatments notes, and basically jump through flaming hoops to keep their clients.

Because of this pendulum swing, scams like this one popped up, where brokers used addicts to bilk insurance companies. Payments for the initial stay in treatment were reasonably easy to justify, so, time after time after time, the scam would recycle "new" clients into another facility. Each time those addicts or alcoholics would get some cash for their trouble, relapse for the weekend, and return to a new facility. Because patients moved from one facility to the next, concurrent reviews to seek the hard-to-get "ongoing care" dollars never were needed. And as for the clients, they never got sober, either.

This was the beginning of my education in rehab scams, but the type and number of them are endless. Utterly naive as I was, I was shocked, at first, at how anyone could take advantage of vulnerable addicts like this. But they do. In fact, an entire industry exists around taking advantage of alcoholics and drug addicts seeking treatment and the families who put so much on the line to help them with interventions. Sometimes, the addicts, who are often scam artists themselves, knowing go along with it (like my three clients). Other times, they have no idea of the scam for which they're being used.

There was even a type of scam meant for those needing intervention, where people who called themselves "interventionists" would talk to families who had a lot of money and/or great insurance policies and tell them they'd send their troubled son or daughter to a really incredible rehab facility. They'd describe the so-called facility, even print out brochures—oh boy, was this a great place for their loved one, with lots of one-on-one attention. So, the families would do the intervention and convince the alcoholic to go away with this strange man to the so-called treatment facility.

Then, as soon as the two of them were on the airplane, the interventionist would get on the phone with five different facilities, trying to sell the client to the highest bidder. That was such a bad scam, it actually hit the news around 2015, but most of these scams are unknown, even to the people victimized by them.

Despite this depressing new information, I had to keep going, so I searched for another, more reliable, client provider. The same medical office that introduced me to the first broker next introduced me to an addiction counselor at a psychiatric hospital in Ohio. You'd think I would have learned not to listen to these guys by this point, but honestly, they were good people and I'm pretty sure they had no idea of the scams these brokers were running—at least, not at first.

The doctors told me they knew this counselor in Indiana who was just banging his head against a brick wall trying to find good treatment facilities in his area. Apparently, there just weren't any quality rehab facilities in the Midwest. In retrospect, I should have looked into that claim, but I didn't. So, I called the counselor, and he sent me referrals. He still charged a fee, but it was far more reasonable than the rehab marketer's had been.

Over the course of three or four months, this counselor sent me twenty-five to thirty insured and authorized clients. We ended up with a pretty full house and everything seemed to be running smoothly. They were a handful of a group, each one, but we were doing the work we were called to do. It felt great. It always takes sixty to ninety days to get insurance reimbursements, though, so I waited patiently and took out loans, in the meantime, to keep the lights on. But eventually, we received a deluge of letters from insurance companies denying all the claims.

As it turned out, the counselor in Indiana was fraudulently signing up all these addicts for insurance, using fake addresses. I don't know who was supposed to pay the premiums, or who made the initial payment, but after the initial payment was made, the payments stopped. The insurance companies considered the policies good, at first, and that's why all my due diligence checked out, but once the payments went into arears, they cancelled the insurance and all payments to rehab. I was out tens of thousands of dollars, maybe more; meanwhile, I had perfectly innocent addicts in my facility that I could not, in good conscience, kick out. They had been bamboozled by the so-called "counselor," as well. In the meantime, I had payroll to make for therapists and counselors of my own, but there was simply no money. I borrowed more. And more. And more.

Things started looking really bleak when I realized the few addicts I helped who actually had legitimate insurance plans weren't in much better shape than those without. These folks were mostly on one of the plans in the Affordable Care Act, which of course are legitimate plans, but not particularly good ones when it comes to mental or behavioral health. Bakersfield is a lower-middle income area, so these people usually had "bronze" level plans—bare bones. At first, I was thrilled to know there was a government program that brought health insurance to so many who needed it, but when I saw what these plans covered, in terms of mental and behavioral health, I was appalled.

Even the best plans had standard deductibles of ten thousand dollars for mental health care. Well, if my clients had ten thousand dollars, they could have self-paid right through rehab if they wanted to. But that's not all. Insurance billing is kind of like California hotel rates, in the sense that facilities who bill insurance have the equivalent of a "rack rate." If you look on the back of a hotel-room door anywhere in California, it tells you the maximum they're allowed to charge for that room. The max might be $400, even though you're only being charged $150 at a cheap motel. With insurance, it kind of works the same. Whatever our fee is, our "rack rate", we will only actually get a small percentage of that, the way the hotel only gets a percentage of its actual rack rate. So, for example, we may have to charge $3000 per night just to end up getting $300. Of course, clients have to meet their own deductibles and copays first, so even that meager payout is only available for those with resources, and only after thirty days of treatment. In most of our cases, the clients couldn't afford the deductible, so this too would have to be absorbed by our facility.

The next problem comes, in most cases, as early as the three-to-six-day mark, when alcoholics still don't know which way is up, but insurance companies call for something called "utilization review." This is where the rehab facility writes a full report on the addict and his progress, definitively demonstrating if and how and why and when the client requires additional days of treatment. The well-known fact that six days is not enough to rehabilitate any alcoholic is not enough for insurance companies. They require rehab clinics to re-prove that fact over and over with every single client. Meanwhile, the case workers must ask for additional days in increments of as little as three days, even though they already know rehab takes sixty to ninety days to have any positive effect. Thus, they must do these utilization reviews again and again and again.

Each unnecessary and redundant utilization review requires a paid case worker, which causes rehab to cost more, even though the insurance companies refuse to acknowledge the extra cost in their pay-outs. Even when they grant additional days, it's often not what's requested but in increments of two or four days at a time. Rehab centers have to tell the addicts about this so they can prepare in case they're forced to pack their stuff and leave, so it's incredibly stressful for the addicts. Gone are the days when folks seeking help could reliably assume they were being admitted for thirty days.

In many cases, addicts simply have no other place to go. Typically, clinics ask them to leave anyway, to make room for the next paying client, but I refused to do that. For me, running this facility was 99% an active aspect of my own recovery and only 1% a way to make a living. As a matter of fact, by a couple of months into running the clinic, I was in debt up to my eyeballs to such a degree that debt almost ceased to have any meaning. It became my policy to let addicts stay in rehab at least sixty days, no matter what, sometimes longer. I'd also make sure they had somewhere to go when they left. No way was I booting my brothers and sisters out to live on the mean streets of Bakersfield or wherever they had come from. So, I kept on borrowing from Brad and Steve to keep the lights on and help the twenty clients I served at any given time, hoping for a miraculous insurance pay-out that, so far, had never come.

Throughout, I borrowed from Peter to pay Paul—telling my insurance biller I'd pay her next week, telling my counselors and case workers their checks were on the way. I made excuses and promises and whatever it took to keep my facility staffed. Everyone was a surprisingly good sport about it, and eventually, insurance checks did end up arriving in the mail. When those precious envelopes arrived, with their distinct cellophane windows and blueish tint to the paper, it was like a holiday—a windfall for everyone! Then, we'd enter another famine phase until the next feast. Throughout it all, I prayed.

CHAPTER NINETEEN

Broke Again, in Bakersfield

By 2018, I had borrowed all I could from Brad and Steve. In addition to losing money by loaning it to me, they had made other questionable business decisions and now they were both in a bad way. We were all in deep trouble in our respective areas, but the money problems didn't draw us together into the three fighting musketeers. Instead, they tore us apart. Steve and Brad had a falling out (probably, in part, because of all the money Brad had suggested loaning me out of their shared coffers). At that point, Steve took the lead on letting me know there would be no more loans, and he began to ask about repayment, too. I wasn't ready for that conversation. But Legacy Village was far from their biggest problem. The main issues between the two of them stemmed from their real estate business and a disgruntled investor who was suing them. To tell the truth, given what I knew of their real estate losses, I was surprised they only had one lawsuit to deal with.

Steve and Brad were brothers-in-law on top of being business partners, and, sadly, the failure of their real estate business was enough to tear that relationship apart, with far-reaching implications. In fact, Steve's side of the family demanded he have nothing more to do with Brad, whom they portrayed as a monster. The pain of their broken relationship was palpable. It was incredibly sad seeing them fall apart like that— business is one thing, but they were family, and family should have come first. At this point, Brad was broke, and his life was falling apart. As for me, I knew I was forever indebted to Brad, in particular, but Steve, also, by extension, for all the faith they'd both shown in my kooky, desperate idea. Yet, what could I do? The checks owed to Legacy Village were still, technically, "in the mail." I did expect to eventually get paid by the insurance companies and get into the black. This was, potentially, a profitable business, it's just that the money took a very long time to come, even after each client's approved treatment had ended.

Then, the disgruntled investor, who knew Legacy Village as the recipient of Brad and Steve's loans, also sued Legacy Village. At that point, I realized Brad and Steve were going to have to deal with their own messes their own way, because now I was alone with mine. I needed a cutthroat business attorney, on the double, and had no idea how to get one.

Steve and his family had resources and, no doubt, business attorneys on retainer. Brad, on the other hand, tried to hide in the shadows, as he had nothing left. As for me, Legacy Village wasn't just a lifeline for my clients but for me, as well. Learning and perfecting the art of staying sober, while also teaching it, was such an all-consuming endeavor, money really didn't mean anything to me. Unfortunately, it meant a lot to my employees and debtors, so I didn't have the luxury of living in some spiritual ivory tower. I was in a weird situation because, despite being financially broke, I still had a lot to lose. Erica and I had built Legacy Village ourselves, with our own two hands. My dad had put in hundreds of hours or more of sweat equity– not for himself, but for me. My mom and sister had come on board, too, in various roles, to keep the dream of Legacy Village alive, usually for little to no pay. In fact, many of the days and months that led to and from this point would have never been possible without my family. So, I needed to save Legacy Village not just for myself, and not just for the clients I treated, but also for my family, which, in a way, had been reunited by this business.

I had just over ten thousand dollars in the bank at that time, which, considering my debts, was a negative amount. Despite our financial burdens, I always tried to keep some money on hand for absolute emergencies, but that abysmal amount was it. Notwithstanding my fear about the money situation, I called around for recommendations and found a business attorney named N. Thomas McCartney who was willing to sit down and have a real talk with me.

He gave me a pretty bleak outlook, considering the lawsuit, all the unofficial loans, and the salaries I owed, but I was glad that at least he was honest. I was a bit turned off by what seemed to be arrogance, though. Mr. McCartney wasn't exactly an emotionally supportive guy, either. He seemed uninterested in all the compelling reasons to keep Legacy Village alive. He was a pessimist, by nature—a consequence of his profession, perhaps— but he was my only chance to rescue the facility. I could renege on all my bills and pay him his initial ten-thousand-dollar retainer, but I didn't know how I'd pay any of his future bills. I didn't mention that in our meeting, although I had a feeling he knew, but he was willing to take me on as a client, anyway, so I went ahead and give him the money ... and hoped for the best.

Mr. McCartney sat down with me and helped me view each one of my casual conversations with Brad and Steve, our emails, and all the loans I'd taken from them, in business terms. He taught me how to write these things down properly. In the process, he was able to help articulate that while Brad and Steve owned the building I used, I had always owned Legacy Village, as a company, outright. I had never given my partners a lien on my company in exchange for the loans. I hadn't, officially, given them anything on paper, so their debtor couldn't actually take the business from me, through them. Setting up the LLC and getting licensed had been the only official, legal proceeding in this entire situation. Other than that, it was all just casual, unsecured loans between friends. Maybe we had IOU's written on scraps of paper someplace, but there wasn't much more documentation than that.

I might still get kicked off this particular piece of real estate, though, which would be devastating. So, while Tom, as I had now begun to call him, strove to straighten out my problems, he also gave me what amounted to a quicky, unofficial MBA as he taught me, by default, how a business is actually supposed to be run. In a sense, he ironed out my money. This time, the ironing wasn't being done for show, nor out of a desperate attempt to have one thing go right in my life. This version of ironing was the real deal: ironing out problems, ironing the wrinkles out of my finances. I finally started to understand how business and money and keeping books and planning for a financial future actually worked. I ironed out the kinks in the haphazard way I'd been living and working. This time, I'd keep my bills flat, facing the same way, and nicely organized—for the long term. With any luck, this was going to be a sea change in my life, and things wouldn't fall apart again.

True to my worries, paying Tom would become problematic. But something interesting happened over the course of this, while past due bills added up. Tom was nearing seventy, but despite our age difference, I really began to consider him a friend, and our conversations became very valuable to me. In time, when his next bill came due, we were able to work out a favorable deal that gave Tom some ownership of Legacy Village. It was, in my opinion, a win-win, since I valued not only his legal work but his advice, counsel, and friendship. Tom remained a pessimist, and I doubt that will change, but today he is still my attorney, and also my friend, and a good one at that.

Tom taught me certain invaluable aspects of legal logic. For instance: Brad and Steve had agreed that as part of our relationship was that they would give me business advice and teach me to spend the money they loaned me properly. That never happened. They were, after all, businessmen, while I was not, yet whenever I received a loan, I was left to my own devices to use it. Their lack of advice, when advice had been promised, was, to Tom, an important aspect of what, so far, amounted to my "failed business." In reality, I didn't blame them for this, but it was a technicality providing another reason why this fourth-party investor couldn't sue me. My attorney was good. Very good!

Throughout all this, Erica and I had finally moved away from the facility, although we were still attending that little church across the street from Legacy Village. That church turned into a real lifeline for us, and the folks there became friends and family. Eventually, they told me about the first time I'd wandered in there, how pathetic and drunk and smelly I'd been. What a lost case I seemed. They had welcomed me, though. That's what they always did. That was their creed. That's literally what they, as a congregation, were there for: folks just like me. Now that I saw people like the man I used to be walk through my doors every day, I understood how they'd had to conceal their disgust and focus on their compassion for me, how they'd had to place hope in a truly hopeless case.

Throughout these troubles, Erica and I were working our steps, including making amends to our families. This is a particularly hard step when the people you "did wrong" were no angels themselves, but that's part of the twelve steps. To succeed, you really have to remove that balance sheet from your mind. The idea where somebody hurt you, so they deserved the hurt you gave them, and then in turn they hurt you again, and you hurt them again… it's a circular game that nobody wins and part of what leads alcoholics to drink. You justify hurting both yourself and others every which way you can, but in the end, your life depends on just accepting that this is a disease that manifests in the form of bad behavior. The bad behavior of others is out of your control, while your own bad behavior is killing you, and only you. Whining about being "done wrong" leads to justifications for drinking, which leads to death. That's why we make amends. No more whining. No more blaming. For recovering addicts, the buck stops with us. It's a hard pill to swallow. For me, the hardest person to make amends to was my father, whom I had always blamed for so many of my problems. Even when I didn't place blame on him, I used his shortcomings as my own justification for wrongdoing.

My Dad, at this point in time, had been hugely instrumental in getting Legacy Village off the ground, although he didn't necessarily know it. He'd done the back-breaking work I didn't have the know-how, time, or money to do. That was one positive trait Dad always had. Furthermore, nowadays, when someone was in need, Dad almost always showed up. For instance, when Brad's world began to fall down, he kept much of it secret, including his family's impending eviction from their apartment. Dad and I only found out with less than twenty-four hours' notice, but Dad leapt into action and moved Brad's family and their things in less than a day. At this point, when I, or any of us, needed Dad, he was there.

Right about this time, Dad received a diagnosis of ocular coronial melanoma: cancer. He had to have an eye removed. Mom and Janee stood by his side the whole time, just as they had always done. And now, I added myself to his support group. Dad had gone through a lot of soul searching in the past few years. That's why, throughout 2017 and 2018, he'd gone out of his way to act as the driver who picked up and dropped off my clients at the airport. Dad was on his own journey of making amends and trying to repair relationships.

When the diagnosis came, for the first time in my life I saw fear in my father— not the cowardly type of fear, but fear of the unknown. He was vulnerable and open to sharing it with me, of all people. He reserved the brave face for Mom and my sister, but with me, he was honest. He had more to do in this life, and he didn't want to die.

It still wasn't easy for me to forgive everything he'd done when I was growing up—the chaotic household we'd had, his betrayals of Mom, his giving the town gossips something to gossip about. After all, if forgiveness was anything other than almost-impossible, I wouldn't have had to hit near-death rock-bottom to do it. That's the nature of the thing. It's hard. But, by now, I had overcome the urge to drink. If I saw an open bottle of wine or a can of beer, I no longer had the urge to take a sip. I just knew this was not for me, just as I wouldn't consider drinking motor oil or dirty dishwater. If I could get to that point, I knew I could get to the point of true forgiveness of Dad.

When they removed his eye, the doctors said there was no guarantee the cancer hadn't spread to other places. It was now a waiting game to see if it popped up someplace else. Life expectancy in cases like these was around five years for those whose cancer had spread. After that, it was likely you were in the clear. If it had spread, there weren't known treatment options for his particular kind of cancer— not very successful ones, anyway. Dad told us that if the cancer came back, he didn't want to know. He was just going to live as long as he lived and not aggravate the situation. He'd seen men go down the depressing, painful path of trying for a cure and die anyway. The lack of options, in a way, helped to prompt his commitment to living with whatever happened, and it gave some resolution. Life is short. That phrase had more meaning now than ever. Dad was only sixty-one when he lost the eye. So, forgiveness and making the amends that came along with that quickly became a now-or-never affair, for me. None of us knew what the future would hold.

When it rains it pours, so right about when I was being sued, when Legacy Village was both successfully helping addicts and being driven into the poor house, when Dad was diagnosed with cancer, when Brad and Steve lost everything and I no longer had a safety net, when my step-daughters were fifteen and nine and now living full time with me and Erica— my own nine-year-old son Anthony was starting to get in trouble at school. I saw it when he spent time with me, too: a really bad attitude, a troubled nature.

Finally, one day, I received an email from him, out of the blue and late at night. When I saw it in my inbox, I was startled, as nine-year-olds aren't typically big on emails. He had never emailed me before. In the message, he begged to come live with me. The poor kid had a choice between his angry stepdad and the mother who sided with him or his alcoholic father who had only recently gone into recovery. A rock and a hard place. Of course, I took him in, and after a very unpleasant discussion of the matter, Ritina agreed to give me full custody. We didn't need to get courts involved.

For me, it was great to have Anthony full-time. It meant I was really in recovery and a full-fledged human being and adult. I had one more person that I couldn't let down. Every time I looked into my son's eyes, it reinforced my determination to make up for all our lost time, together. Erica, of course, embraced him as her own son, and the five of us became a full-time family. As for Emily, she was happy in her home with Elizabeth, where she had two new baby brothers, so I continued to see her on weekends and summers, and that seemed to be best for everyone.

Selfishly, I would have liked to have Emily live with Erica and me, too, but you don't just get to go into recovery, rejoin the land of the living, and claim everything you've left behind. While you're drunk and half-dead living on Pismo Beach, ex-wives move on, children grow up, the world keeps turning, and if you ever manage to go into recovery, you're lucky if you get any scraps of your old life back. I was lucky. I got a lot more back than many alcoholics. A lot more.

CHAPTER TWENTY

In Service to Our Country

Bobby was a Vietnam veteran in his sixties— an alcoholic with a heart condition who had been living on the streets of Bakersfield for years, maybe decades. He finally decided, one day in 2019, that he was ready to dry out and improve his life. There was no V.A. facility in Bakersfield for rehab, but there was a van veterans could catch at 6:00 am that would take them two hours to the V.A. in West Los Angeles and bring them back at 4:00 pm. So, Bobby hopped on the van on a Friday morning, got to the V.A., told them his situation, and asked for help.

The V.A. agreed to admit Bobby, but he'd have to wait for some paperwork to go through, so he sat in the waiting room all day, and then about 6:30 that night, they told him they wouldn't be able to admit him, after all. He'd have to come back on Monday. Trouble was, the van to Bakersfield had already left. The V.A. told him he couldn't stay inside the facility for the weekend. They didn't have a place for him, and so Bobby spent the next couple of nights sleeping on the street outside the hospital, just biding his time, waiting for the van to return on Monday. I'm not sure exactly what happened the following Monday, but it was nothing good.

It was then that one of my employees came to me, asking for a favor. He told me about his friend Bobby, how motivated he was to get well and how the V.A. had failed him. Naturally, I told him if Bobby was willing to come in, we'd take care of him. That's what we were there for.

I hoped it wouldn't be a complete charity case, as veterans are insured, after all, but I had never dealt with the V.A. before. At the end of the day, my desire to treat those in need wasn't changed by the fact of us needing to be paid for those services. (If only my creditors would agree!)

We admitted Bobby to Legacy Village, then applied for an authorization from the V.A., which we never got, even after ninety days of constant entreaties and requests. Trying to get the V.A. to cooperate felt like banging our heads against a wall, and we eventually gave up, called Bobby's full, ninety-day treatment a scholarship, and left the financial part of it at that. In rehab, "scholarship" is normally something where a benevolent third party leaves money to help others. In our case, it meant we treated the client for free.

Bobby took to recovery wonderfully.

He ended up getting and staying sober, landing a small job, finding his own little place to live, and experiencing true happiness and stability. He was the type of client that reassures me Legacy Village is really able to make a long-lasting difference in peoples' lives. Sadly, Bobby died from health complications about a year and a half after getting sober, but near to his death, he told me the last two years of his life had been better than the previous twenty.

Knowing Bobby and everything he had been through got the gears turning in my head. There were probably a lot of Bobbies out there. Those who lived in outlying areas, like Bakersfield, where there was no specialty care at the Veterans Administration, were all going to have trouble getting access to help, just like he had. The V.A. really needed to do better by these men and women. So, I looked into the situation and what I learned quickly overwhelmed me. In many some respects, it seemed like mental and behavioral healthcare were new to the V.A. Addicted veterans were massively underserved in their system. In fact, I learned that the number of veterans committing suicide was anywhere from twenty-two to forty-four per day! There were no statistics on how many of those were addicts, but I guessed it was a lot.

I called the V.A. and talked to a few different people with authority, telling them about our facility in Bakersfield. I let them know we were open for business and eager to treat the veterans who seemed to need our services so badly. As a result, I got some advice on the right way to bill for these types of clients and also a couple of referrals. So, our next couple of veterans came in 2019, and we actually got paid for them. Things were looking up, both financially and ethically, in terms of my ability to reach out to those in need whom I could really help. With these veteran clients, we began to hit a stride and get paying clients on a consistent basis.

Then, COVID-19 hit. You'd flip on the TV and people were dying everywhere. Nobody wanted to be in an old folks' home. Nobody wanted to go to a hospital. People were no longer attending twelve-step meetings. Every type of residential treatment center was looking at death counts, and Legacy Village emptied out quicker than you could say, "I saw it on the evening news." My wife and I started having groceries delivered and spraying them with Lysol before bringing them in the house. No one knew what this pandemic was all about or what would happen next.

To say we were living paycheck to paycheck gives an idea of our financial situation but isn't exactly accurate, as the paychecks didn't come in any predictable manner. Sometimes we'd have windfalls where the mailbox would be literally stuffed with checks from various insurance agencies, and other times, we'd go weeks or months without a single one. We were raising three kids in the midst of this, and when they asked for things, we never actually knew if we could afford it. Would we get a check tomorrow? Who knows? They learned to stop asking, and it broke my heart. To get through it all, we prayed. We prayed a lot. Insurance payments were so unpredictable that, sometimes, praying while waiting was truly the only thing left to do.

By the time April of 2020 rolled around, we had no clients left—logically, they all figured life on the streets or in an alcoholic stupor was better than dying horribly from the COVID germs spread in a residential treatment facility. I couldn't blame them. No one knew how dangerous COVID was or how much more deadly it would get, and there were no readily available answers. It felt like an apocalypse for Erica and me—not just the presence of the deadly virus, but the fact that it made alcoholism impossible to treat. Finally, I had to close my doors.

I met with my employees and laid out the situation: they could go on unemployment and get paid very close to what they'd been making with me, so being laid off was not actually going to be a very big financial hit for them. In fact, I was the only one who'd have to suffer in this situation. They had all been with me for the past four and a half years we'd been open. We were a tightly bonded group of really caring people, so they were sad about the center closing but all agreed to go gently into the good night of our COVID shut down.

After they left, I sat in my office chair and lit a cigarette. You can't smoke inside, anywhere in California, so this was a no-no, but under the circumstances, who really cared? As the smoke trailed up and spread over the room, I looked around. I was sitting in my office, which used to be the kitchen of the apartment I'd been living in when I went to rehab for the last time. This was the very place where I'd had my last drink.

Drinking Dennis would have been depressed in this situation. Drinking Dennis would have laid into the booze like there was no tomorrow, but strangely, Sober Dennis didn't take it that hard. For the past four and a half years, I had faced one financial crisis after another and seen each of them "miraculously" resolved. I don't use the word "miraculous" lightly. It's not exactly right, but it's also not exactly wrong.

What had gotten Erica and me through the financial insecurity of our sober lives was, very simply, the deep belief that we were doing the right thing, God's work. It was no fun to not be able to buy things for your kids or to skimp and save even while working sixty to eighty hours per week. The lifestyle we'd developed at Legacy Village was insane, but it gave our lives purpose, every single day. It kept us sober not just by keeping us busy, but by making us feel like we mattered, our work mattered, and our sobriety mattered to a lot of people. Now that my clients were gone, it's logical to think I might feel as if I no longer mattered... but I didn't.

Somehow, I just knew everything was going to be okay. I attribute this to the depth of the faith I had built over the past four and a half years. I simply believed, very deeply, that God had a plan for me. I believed that putting myself in His hands through prayer and surrendering myself to his guidance would always lead me to the right place. This had worked throughout the last, topsy-turvy four and a half years, and this moment, though more extreme than usual, was really no different.

Numbers-wise, we were owed months' worth of insurance payments at this point—around $280,000 to $300,000. We often didn't get payments such as these, and under the current circumstances, I guessed we'd never see a penny of it. Still, I knew that whatever happened, I wouldn't go back to starving to death on Pismo Beach. No matter what, that was not on the menu, so how bad could things get, really? It was all a matter of perspective. I locked up the office with a view to leaving it that way indefinitely and walked around the building for a nostalgic glance around before driving home.

I spent the next week as if on vacation. Part of why I was so relaxed was probably the fact that the reality of my situation hadn't fully sunk in, yet. I think I was a little bit in denial, a little bit trusting in God, a little bit blind to the facts of life in 2020. It was a combination of all those things that got me through the following week relatively emotionally unscathed.

On day ten of being closed, I opened up the mailbox and found $244,000 worth of checks. They all arrived the same day. Divine intervention? Maybe. I don't discount that. It also might have been the fact that the insurance workers had been relieved of other jobs because of COVID, so they finally got around to paying these bills. In any case, I looked Heavenward in thanks, did a happy dance, and ran home to tell Erica. We were in the black, again!

I knew my workers were being taken care of by unemployment insurance, by now, so I was free to use the money to pay some outstanding bills of my own. I didn't want to let the utilities get turned off and have things degenerate to the point where we couldn't open again when things turned around. Against all odds, I felt it was important to stay ready to reopen, just in case.

A week later, I got a phone call from the Veterans Administration up in Fresno, a couple hours north of Bakersfield. They told me they'd had a couple of guys go through Legacy Village and they really liked what we were doing. In fact, numerous veterans in need of this type of care had expressed a desire for a recovery center just for veterans, where they could be among their own. "Would you ever be interested in treating only veterans?" he asked, adding that, if so, he had a backlog of clients for me.

I took a deep breath. It was all I could do to remain calm and professional. I decidedly didn't tell them my facility was closed. I simply said it was something I'd take under consideration and "talk to my team about it." After hanging up the phone, I jumped around the room like a leprechaun on fire, shouting "Thank you, God! Thank you, God!"

Then, I called all the employees, one by one. They had been out of work and enjoying their unemployment benefits for a few weeks, now. I didn't know if they'd be willing to come back, under the circumstances. So, I just told them what had been asked of us—that there were veterans in need who required our help. Were they game to come back to work and help put together a program especially for veterans?

Every single person said yes.

CHAPTER TWENTY-ONE

Wellness Center

Legacy Village reopened in May of 2020 and was at half capacity within a month. This time, I had no more hassles with multiple insurance companies, as I dealt only with the V.A. This felt pretty risky to me. My track record so far with them had been hit and miss, but I trusted God to help me help those in need. As long as I was doing the work I now knew I'd been put on this Earth for, I had faith that my family would be taken care of, one way or another.

After a couple of months being open under these new circumstances, it became clear we were playing a whole different ball game, now. The V.A. gave every client thirty to forty-five days of treatment right out of the gate. There were no more ridiculous utilization reviews at days four and eight and ten and fifteen, and so on. This way, I knew, my employees knew, our therapists and doctors knew, and most importantly, the clients themselves knew that we were definitely going to make progress. Morale increased a thousand-fold.

I now know that sixty to ninety days is the bare minimum for a true, long-lasting foundation of recovery. After all, the first thirty days goes by in a whirlwind. That month is about wiping the cobwebs away, clearing the slate. It's just the first step, then comes the real work. Luckily, the performance reviews we had to do at thirty or forty-five days were pretty perfunctory, and it became relatively easy to get the V.A. to extend client stays to sixty or even ninety days. Hallelujah! Real work could be done!

Clients now had a real sense of living at Legacy Village, enjoying our communal space, gathering for twelve-step meetings, settling into their rooms. They weren't living under threat of eviction every few days, and that made a huge difference to their state of mind. While all alcoholics have certain things in common, they are people, not cardboard cut-outs, and each one has a unique reason to drink and keep drinking. Most of the veterans came to us with co-occurring conditions, too. We dealt with guys that had PTSD and high blood pressure and heart conditions right along with their alcoholism and/or drug addiction. This meant we now needed to provide more and more care from trained medical and other professionals. It meant we were growing!

By July, we were at full capacity, the checks were rolling in predictably, and, to my great surprise, Legacy Village was actually making a profit. Meanwhile, outside our walls, the pandemic raged on. We took care to keep everything as COVID safe as possible, testing people upon entry and not allowing visitors, so we became what people were calling a "pod" of our own. The isolation required for recovery actually meshed well with the entire COVID shut-down situation, once we got the clients inside the walls.

By August, I understood that what was happening here was no flash in the pan. As far as I know, we were (and still are) one of the only rehab facilities in the country catering exclusively to veterans. The V.A. was just as grateful to us as we were to them. I couldn't believe that right in the middle of COVID, Legacy Village was not only growing but growing fast. Once we started to generate a waiting list, I knew it was time to make some improvements.

Our location had been a great one for a rehab center, at first, largely because it was the only building I had access to. Also, Bakersfield has plenty of alcoholics, so, being located in the absolute worst part of town, we were basically in the thick of it. However, being in the thick of it brought its own set of problems. For instance, you could walk out our doors and score a prostitute, heroin, cocaine, whatever you wanted. Having those two liquor stores across the street (the ones Erica and I used to consider our grocery stores) didn't help, either. Typically, the clients who came to our facility stayed behind our gate and didn't leave the whole time, so this wasn't too bad of a problem, but if I was going to improve anything about Legacy Village (since I now had the resources to do it), it would be the location.

It was true enough that Erica and I didn't want to raise our kids in the ghetto, and while we had moved away from the facility some time ago, we were still close by. I also wanted to bring my clients somewhere that gave them hope. I wanted grass and trees and a sense of spaciousness for them, not the current sense of being "confined to quarters" inside our tiny concrete compound. Alcoholics already feel like they don't deserve better than the dregs. In truth, a lot of addicts considered our two little buildings paradise compared to the circumstances they'd come from, but I wanted to provide something even better.

With everything at the center running like a top, now, I had the luxury of time, so I spent it seeking out a new location. First, I searched Bakersfield, itself. I had been thinking we wouldn't have to move far to find something in a nicer neighborhood with a bit of a backyard, but it wasn't that easy, especially with zoning issues around a facility like mine. So, I expanded my search to all of Kern County. Eventually, I came across a Zillow listing for a house on a nice piece of acreage about an hour and a half west of Bakersfield. This was still close enough to Fresno not to cause inconvenience for the Veterans Administration there, but boy was it a different location. I drove out there to meet the owner and, I mean, it was positively bucolic. Twenty-five acres of trees, meadows ... basically, paradise.

When I talked to the owner, I found out there were two homes on the property, about 7,000 square feet apiece. Perfect. One had a big room that would be idea for our "group room." There would be very little renovation needed for us to simply move the facility right onto the property, but the trouble was, the owner only wanted to lease one of the houses while he lived in the other one. I had misunderstood his advertisement. I explained to him that with a rehab facility, it has to be completely controlled. Nobody else can come in and out of the gates. We can't have a "civilian" living on the grounds. Besides which, I didn't think he'd particularly enjoy living next to a rehab - where at first, clients shuffle into the facility looking like victims of a zombie apocalypse. Oh, well. I thanked him for his time.

The fellow said he'd think about all this and get back to me. Then, the very next day, he called and told me yes. He'd lease me the entire place, both houses, and for an amount that was far less than what I expected. I heartily agreed and did my happy dance! But then reality started to creep in. My staff—who had all been with me between four and five years, were not likely to be willing to commute or move out to the Central Coast. It was an expensive place to live, unlike Bakersfield.

First, I talked to the clinical staff, the counselors and therapists, and asked if they had any interest in moving. It would be a wonderful environment to work in, but with the expense of the move and new grounds, even increases to their salaries may not be enough. I didn't want to lose these people. They were an essential part of the company. I also owed them, big time, after they'd been so cooperative about going on unemployment and then coming back to work when they really didn't have to. Luckily, almost all of them chose to move with us!

Next, I had to talk to my entry-level people. Minimum wage was eight or nine bucks an hour, but I paid twelve to thirteen, so this was a pretty good gig for them, but who moves an hour and a half away for a low-wage job like that? I didn't expect these folks to stick with me. I supposed I could have replaced them, but I really didn't want to—partly because we Legacy Village workers were a family, together. Understanding rehab clientele and the needs of our environment was important, even for the kitchen workers and maintenance crew, and my people did a great job. In the end, those who could, came, and those who couldn't knew they would always be considered part of something special. Legacy Village remains the only place I've worked where ex-employees regularly come back to visit.

So, things went forward. I inked the deal with the property owner and started the process of transferring our treatment license to the new location. With the new school year about to start, Erica and I decided to go ahead and move the family, first. I'd commute back and forth to Bakersfield until the facility was ready to move.

It took four or five months to clean up and prepare the property, and in the meantime, the pandemic raged on. It was a sad state of affairs for America (and the world), but for us, we were just moving our "pod" from one location to another, so we stayed pretty safe. It was confusing, too, because by this point, I also had misgivings as to how serious the situation really was. The months spent preparing gave me a lot of time to think about what else, besides a new location, I could do to improve Legacy Village—to put a special stamp on our program and make it even better.

Personally, I had dried out using the traditional Alcoholics Anonymous, twelve-step system. It works, eventually. Addicts have to be motivated, of course, and work their steps with diligence, but that's the nature of any recovery. It isn't something that is done to you, but something where once you learn how, you have to take the reins and do it yourself, with guidance. I had been running Legacy Village on that same model, so far, and it was working well.

Philosophically, however, I felt like there was something missing. One thing I knew about myself as an addict was that once I cemented my relationship with God, I felt my body getting healthier. Then, when Erica came back to me, my son came back to me, and I made peace with my father, I felt so much better than I had ever felt before. I also educated myself, mostly through those talks with my business attorney who was now a full-fledged friend. As such, I started actually making a living. I hadn't quit cigarettes yet, but it was on my to-do list. I had so much overall wellness at this point, that it made me want to see how far I could take it. A big part of every situation where people are self-destructing is that they just don't have enough to live for in the first place. My permanent recovery wasn't simply due to the absence of alcohol but the presence of essential, positive things in the spiritual, physical, and emotional realms that made me into someone who would never ever even consider taking another drink again. Now, I had too much to lose.

The name I gave to the positive, forward-looking aspect of my recovery is "wellness." I wanted to integrate that even more into Legacy Village. Not only would my clients learn what they needed to *stop* doing, and a new lifestyle they needed to *adopt*, they needed to truly *heal*, along with their families, until, like me, they ended up with so much to live for that turning back wasn't even tempting.

Thus, I swapped out our old sign, "Legacy Village Recovery Centers" for a new one: "Legacy Village Wellness Centers." When we moved to the new location, I talked to our therapists about adding additional components to our work. I wanted them to look at a four-pronged healing regimen including:

- Physical health
- Mental health
- Emotional health
- Spiritual health

The therapists liked the four-pronged idea as well as the unique addition of looking at education and employment as facets of health. After all, without these, it's pretty hard to keep up with the other health components. These six items were, in fact, areas the therapists were already addressing, but they liked having this somewhat formalized method for looking at each item. Over time, to serve these needs, I took on additional therapists and outside facilitators such as a retired professional surfer who served as a "surf therapist" to deal with clients' physical needs, help them get used to taking risks in a sober setting, and get them out of their troubled minds and into their bodies.

We also set up group therapy sessions to rehabilitate clients' relationships with family members. More than anyone, I know about how addiction is a family disease. Even if there is only one alcoholic in the family, that person burns bridges with family members over and over and over, which creates a lot of conflict and impacts everyone in a different way. The conflict they cause, the financial problems, the ethical and moral quandaries, and the emotional challenges can absolutely tear a family apart, even if nobody else is an addict. It's important for a recovering addict to understand what they put their loved-ones through with their lifestyle choices, so we create therapy sessions where they are asked to confront these facts.

With me, for instance, even when I wasn't around, my parents suffered from knowing I was in perpetual danger. Even though their own lives were never particularly stable, they still worried about me. For a lot of addicts, when they hear how their loved ones suffer, they don't agree the suffering was their fault. That's okay. They don't have to agree. They just have to know the other person's viewpoint. So much human conflict is based upon the notion that people have to agree in order to get along, but they really don't. They just need to be heard. Agreement may or may not come, in time. You can't rush the process, but you can't even participate in the process unless you start the conversation, open lines of communication, and stop keeping alcoholism as a "family secret."

We got clients started with online classes, too, where they could learn a new career or update skills in their old ones. When our veterans left Legacy Village, we wanted them to have somewhere to go, gainful employment when they got there, loving (or at least accepting) relationships for support, and a deep sense that their "higher power" would not let them down. That, to me, was the main thing, because realizing God was actually *on my side* had been the biggest game changer of all.

Most veterans come to us with co-occurring disorders, too, so they have PTSD, anxiety, depression, heart problems, blood pressure issues— so many things. Most alcoholics in rehab probably also have these other problems, too, but if they're like me, they never went to a doctor, never got diagnosed, and had to wait until well after rehab to deal with all the other stuff, separately. With veterans, though, once they get into the system, it's pretty thorough, so not only our counselors but also the psychiatrists we have on staff now can help with clients' anxiety and depression while helping them dry out. The team we now have on staff deal with their physical issues—we handle it all.

I have really enjoyed the whole-self approach I've been able to use with these veterans because of the V.A.'s cooperation. I only wish other insurance carriers had the foresight to help addicts in this holistic way. In the long run, it would save them money on innumerable aspects of health care, but most insurance just isn't set up to treat the whole person. I think that's a well-known fact in America, but running a rehab facility has certainly brought it to my direct attention on a daily basis.

CHAPTER **TWENTY-TWO**

Legacy Village Today

A s I write this book, Legacy Village has achieved an unheard-of low rate of recidivism. As I mentioned before, most addicts dry out like I did—after three or more attempts. With each attempt, we addicts take the process more seriously, but after each attempt, we relapse and sink lower and lower until we find entirely new definitions of "rock bottom." The lucky ones, like me, finally figure it out, find something to live for, and realize that while some people can handle a pleasant cocktail at the end of a hard day, for others, that's the road to hell. Others never make it out— a sad reality in my world.

Call it bad luck, a trick of genetics, or a multi-car emotional pile-up, but the fact that alcoholism is an honest-to-God disease is something alcoholics take a lot of time to accept. Most of us never thought of ourselves as "sick," before and find it very hard to accept that we have something wrong with us—something incurable. I know this very well, because, of course, I am an alcoholic. So, helping people understand that rehab isn't just "a break" is baked into the program I run, here. We examine the things in clients' lives that are lacking, that are driving them to drink or use in the first place, and we try to fix those things before clients leave. We also know that:

1. We aren't going to "fix" anyone. It's up to them.
2. Any remedy that occurs while a veteran is with us is a foundation, not the full cure.

In fact, regardless of the methodology any rehab center adopts, there is no "cure" for addiction. Our sobriety is entirely based on regular maintenance. Legacy Village is helped in this, now, by the sense of camaraderie that already exists among veterans.

Over the years, our facility has become co-ed, with men and women segregated, although we see far more men than women. This has its pitfalls, though. In talking about how I met Erica, in previous chapters, I mentioned the phenomenon known as "thirteenth stepping," where alcoholics or addicts date one another and believe they're falling in love, but it's often just another way to divert the mind from the work of recovery. For Erica and me, the love turned out to be real, but we are actually in the minority with that. So, when we began to admit women, we did notice that relationships in the community became more complicated than what may be conducive to recovery. I do hope, however, that we can someday open up a Legacy Village just for women, because, as far as I know, there is currently no recovery center dedicated to female veterans, and they certainly deserve to have the same sense of camaraderie in their recovery that the guys have, here.

Because we no longer have to waste innumerable resources on dealing with insurance companies, we have been able to help people much more reliably than before, which makes me happy but also sad about all the addicts whose recovery is held back by insurance policies that seem to treat rehab like it's a vacation they don't want to pay for. After all, anyone who has gone through rehab can attest to the fact that it is no vacation. Anyone who needed to get to rehab can attest that being in active addiction is no vacation, either.

This is why I never stop trying to improve the program. We currently serve twelve clients at a time, but we've bought ten acres where we're going to build our own facility that will serve up to twenty-two clients. Once we do that, we'll have things down to a science well enough that we can replicate what we do here. While I would love to see our program re-engage with the general public, I have little hope for massive improvement from insurance companies. For now, we're sticking with the Veterans Administration for so many reasons, but if the healthcare system in

America were to fundamentally change, I'd be thrilled to be able to include a wider variety of clients in this type of holistic treatment.

As I mentioned, it is well known that, in America, twenty-two veterans die by suicide per day. That's the statistic put out by the V.A. But, according to some media reports, it's actually closer to forty-five. And eighty percent of those can be traced back to some type of mental or behavioral health diagnosis, which often includes substance abuse. It's simple math: rehab facilities save lives. The lower the recidivism rate, the more lives they save.

Statistics also state that two out of every ten rehab clients stay sober for a year. That's twenty percent—a terrible rate. At Legacy Village we average a fifty-four percent success rate. We know this because we follow up with clients. Our clients are family, and everyone on staff is emotionally invested in their continued good health. In fact, we have events for our alumni. They return and talk to current clients about how much this work has helped them, even saved their lives. This kind of ongoing care inspires people quite a bit and reminds them of the diligence needed to remain sober in a world filled with temptation.

I mention this to make note of the fact that doing rehab from a holistic perspective is more than just the included elements of wellness, providing unusual therapies, offering family counseling, and all of that. It's also a matter of healing from the past while looking into the future. Seeing the futures that other clients have built for themselves is a big part of that. In AA, they say, "We share what we have through attraction, not promotion," which is a way of saying we don't have to go out and proselytize. People look at you, even people who didn't know you were an alcoholic, and they say, "Something's different. What's different?" That's when we have a chance to tell people about our journey and sometimes a chance to express a newfound belief in God. In my opinion, the same opportunity exists with my Christianity. I hope to inspire people to ask, "What's different?" about me or anyone who has found God, not because I hit anyone over the head with it – but because they can see it. It doesn't always bring others into the fold, but getting our message out there is a matter of living sober and letting attraction do the work for you.

In the beginning, I wasn't able to provide all these things. In fact, I used to not know from month to month if the center was even going to stay open, but since we've allied with the Veterans Administration, we've had both the funds and the manpower freed up to do these things.

The way insurance companies used to make the rehab business a living hell is a thing of the past for Legacy Village, but very much a present-day situation for most rehab centers out there, and it really stands in the way of recovery. It also discourages the workers, counselors, and administrators at the centers, who are working under the umbrella of "health" agencies who show no actual human caring about anyone's health. In short, the frequent, insurance-required performance reviews threaten clients' well-being. They cost lives.

Before worrying about reimbursement was a thing of the past for us, we treated a lot of clients for free. Usually, we just didn't know if we were getting paid or not, until the treatment was over, but in any case, the people in question were real alcoholics or addicts. They were simply being exploited by scammers. My belief in God and living right, doing the right thing, made me help those people just like the others and see them through their recovery. A good test of any career, after all, is—do you love it so much, you'd do it for free? Well, I have done it for free, so, yes, and I'm sure I'll help more people like that if and when the Lord asks me to.

Interestingly, we've kept in touch with about a dozen clients from the Indiana scam who stayed in California and are still clean and sober and attending our alumni events. I'm not bitter about the frauds that used them because they tested my faith. I think I passed that test, which is a testament to my own recovery, which is still, of course, at the center of all this. More than anything, I don't want Legacy Village to earn anything off of being a revolving door. My mission here is to rehabilitate individuals for good, not to make money from seeing them return again and again. If they don't return as alumni, I hope it's because they have entirely new lives now and don't need us anymore, which is the best outcome I could hope for.

At this point, the Lord has blessed me with a good living from the work I do, and I strongly believe it's because I'm following a righteous path. Don't get me wrong: it isn't me that's righteous but my faith in Jesus that's covered me in His righteousness. An important distinction. I do love having a successful business, though. It's nice living in a nice house in a great part of the world, raising my kids in gorgeous surroundings and finally being able to buy them the things they need and ensure their educations well into the future. The benefits of Legacy Village to me and my family have been enormous, but I've seen enough ups and downs over the years to know God gives no guarantees. So, I keep working for the people at Legacy Village, improving the center, praying for guidance, and trying to ensure my staff here maintains the same high level of commitment and integrity they have always shown.

CHAPTER TWENTY-THREE

Traits

Once I made Legacy Village into what I call a "wellness center," as opposed to simply a rehab, I was thrilled that so many of my long-time employees were willing to move with me to the central coast. As a result, I spent some time asking myself what was so special about these counselors, therapists, food service workers, doctors, maintenance people, technicians, and other employees. Their work ranges from simple to highly skilled labor, and they're all good at what they do, but, to be honest, I have found it isn't that hard to find employees who are good at their jobs. What's difficult, and what I somehow achieved early on with God's help, is finding people who have the right attitude for the work, whose whole hearts are invested in healing.

After all, a lot of the veterans we help here have been through the wringer, and they're not exactly cute and cuddly. A lot of them are like I was when I bumbled into my last detox program, drunk as a skunk, feeling utterly hopeless, and depressed to have lost (or so I thought) yet another loving spouse because of my addiction. When clients come to us, they're at their worst, which doesn't just mean they have treated themselves badly. It also means they have treated others badly and very well may continue to do so while at Legacy Village. Thinking you're better than those trying to help you and superior to other alcoholics is, in fact, a common symptom of the disease of alcoholism. When I see clients behaving this way, it doesn't offend me. It brings out compassion, instead—not because I'm some kind of superior, ultra-zen human being.

Far from it. It's simply that I've been there. I see myself in them. I know these people need my help, and most of all, I know they need God's help.

The first step in the Alcoholics Anonymous twelve-step system has nothing to do with faith, though. It is accepting that your use of alcohol has made your life unmanageable. Typically, every rehab client has achieved this, or they wouldn't have come to rehab in the first place. Although, in the outside world, when alcoholics are living from one drink to the next but still keeping a job, a relationship, and a life together, they are still in denial of step one. All it takes is a little extra drinking or one thing in their carefully managed lives to go sideways, and people at this level finally realize that walking a tight rope is not actually a manageable life. This brings them to the all-important step two.

Step two is acknowledging that a power greater than yourself can restore you to sanity. This was tough for me, so I sympathize when I meet other alcoholics who simply do not believe in God. A tough life has shown them that there is no mercy, there is no grace, there is nobody out there keeping an eye on them and protecting them. Veterans of war have seen worse things than even your typical alcoholics, and many of them, who once had faith in God, lost it when they witnessed atrocities. All I can do to help clients along this path is show them the love God has put in my soul to give. Witnessing horrors strips the soul of any sense of being loved by a higher power, any sense that there is order to the universe, so restoring faith is a simple matter, I think, of overwhelming those bad memories with good, loving ones. Rehab is a strict process, but there's a big difference between administering strict policies according to some rule book and administering them out of love.

This brings me back to the qualities shown by my best employees. I have actually taken the trouble to quantify them. This is in order to make folks aware of them so they can build upon them but also as a way of letting new applicants know what sort of employees we're looking for, here. What I really want to tell people is that love should permeate everything they do at Legacy Village. Our goal is to restore clients' faith in themselves, God, and the world at large, and to bring them into God's love. However, I can't require anyone to "love" anyone, which, ironically, is the same (and only) limitation God has. What I can do, though, is break down the components of how love is expressed. If employees are behaving according to these components, then for all intents and purposes, they are behaving in a loving way. It all begins with being of service—that's the work of Legacy Village. We spend our lives being of service in one very specific way to one very specific population of people (addicts and alcoholics). In order to be of service, everyone employed here needs to embody certain traits.

Honesty, Awareness, and Integrity

The first set of traits is *honesty*, *awareness*, and *integrity*. I define honesty as the act of communicating facts to clients, rather than your personal beliefs. Clients don't need pep talks all about some pie-in-the-sky life they're going to lead once they leave here. It would not be honest to tell them rehab will be easy and life as a recovering addict will be a piece of cake. Addicts don't need to showered with sunshine and imaginary unicorns. They need to know what they're up against. They need to know the truth, so honesty from my employees at Legacy Village is key.

I pair the trait of honesty with that of awareness, which is the act of observing the world in order to discern objective truth. This brings us back again to truth, facts, reality—not fanciful ideals. Close observation of clients and what they talk about helps my team provide the best care possible. Accordingly, close observation of client progress through the program helps the team ease up on aspects of recovery the client has mastered and push them harder in the more difficult ones. One simply cannot be honest and therefore helpful unless one has a consistent, ongoing practice of observing the world for the reality it presents.

Integrity is essential to both honesty and awareness, as it determines what you will do when faced with certain harsh realities. If you have a client that you have observed to be rebellious, or even if you have a client that's very docile, you must always use integrity in choosing the right action to help that person based upon the reality of his life. After all, there are those who use the truths they know in order to manipulate people. That's honesty and awareness being used for evil. Rehab is not manipulation. Nobody here is forced to recover. It's a choice that must be made by the addict, so those who have observed and understood the truth of our clients' lives must use integrity as they present them with those truths and the choices the clients consequently face.

Hope, Faith, and Humility

The next set of traits is hope, faith, and humility. Sometimes people think the idea of having hope contrasts too much with life's reality for both "honesty" and "hope" to be uttered on the same page. And yet, maintaining an understanding of life's harsh truths while also believing things can get better is at the heart of rehabilitation. Hope means believing *and acting* as if your goal is achievable. If you believe clients can recover, you will, quite simply, act that way. The tone of your voice will imply hope. Your speech will neither ooze with sympathy nor resound with false encouragement. You set the example of having hope by simply and truly behaving as one does when they have hope.

Faith is the belief that you are not the only actor in your life. It is an understanding that a power higher than yourself factors into your achievements. Faith is the key to hope, for many of us. If you believe that a higher power loves you and will help you if only you help yourself, then you hold out hope for your life to improve.

There is a reason we say "higher power" instead of "God" in rehab, when referring to faith, because even if your viewpoint is not a religious one or even a spiritual one, any rational person must acknowledge that many things are out of your control. You can call those things coincidences, accidents, luck-of-the-draw, the laws of probability, fortune smiling on you, Murphy's Law, or any of the millions of reasons people give for things happening that they can't control. For instance, for many people, alcoholism is a genetic disease. You can say the disease was given to you by God or you can just call it bad luck. It doesn't matter what you call it—genetics and God are both out of your control, either way.

Acknowledgement that certain things are out of your control is one of the keys to recovery, because in many cases, alcoholism is a disease about trying to control your mood, at all times. The most difficult aspect of this understanding is having faith that the "higher power" in question is a good and benevolent one. Some people come into recovery believing in some version of the devil and no version of God. That's simply the conclusion they've drawn from the events of their lives. Our job here, as I see it, is to show them the love that lets them know their higher power is a good one, and that is a function of the act of having faith, which, in turn, instills faith in others.

I define humility as the willingness to execute the work that is required by hope and faith, no matter the discomfort. Sure, if you believe in yourself and you believe in God, it seems like good things should fall into your lap, doesn't it? But when circumstances require you to do something difficult or embarrassing or harsh to achieve your goals, can you? Or are you sitting around expecting hope and faith to take care of things for you? Humility is exercised by the workers here who have to clean puke up of the floor and make meals for addicts whose behavior is less than friendly. Humility lies at the heart of everything we do at Legacy Village, as its opposite, pride, would prevent any of us from even showing up to do this difficult work.

Courage and Self Discipline

Courage is taking action in the face of fear. Fear is something I think everyone can relate to. All of us can recall some situation where we felt fear and look back upon how we responded. If we faced it and moved through the fear to achieve a situation where the fear went away, that was courageous. But if we shrank from the fear and refused to engage with it … not so much. Sometimes, fear can be a very useful emotion that tells you not to do something incredibly dangerous, and shrinking away from the fearful situation is the right and safe action. But for alcoholics, the issue of fear ties into our need for control. When a fearful situation occurs, an alcoholic will typically respond by drinking himself into a stupor, which is the opposite of facing the fear.

When you have courage, it really doesn't matter what action your courage leads you to take. In the beginning of sobriety, you might take too much action … or too little. If you've never experienced being courageous while sober, before, it takes some getting used to. That's why the team at Legacy Village need to embody that courage in everything they face—whether on our grounds or off—because when you're brave, generally speaking, as a person, it shows through everything you do.

When I say self-discipline, I also mean self-awareness in the mind, body, and spirit. Such self-discipline enables one to be courageous, which is why I pair these traits together. Without the self-discipline to do what's right, it's impossible to be courageous, and without the courage to stand up against peers or other bad influences, one cannot exercise the self-discipline required to abstain from drinking.

Patience and Perseverance

Finally, I ask my employees to consider the qualities of patience and perseverance in their own lives and at work. Patience is a matter of confronting obstacles with a calm, problem-solving demeanor. It doesn't mean sitting around waiting for someone else to take action, nor is patience a matter of sitting by while you see someone else take wrong action. In a rehab facility, we have to have patience with our clients but not with their addictions. We do not want to patiently watch clients refuse to participate in programing and fail to open up in therapy sessions. That would not be patience— it would be apathy. We do, however, want to hold space for them as we watch them make gradual progress. Nobody is expected to spring into recovery instantly. It takes time.

Perseverance is defined as the willingness to exercise patience until a goal is achieved, which is why patience and perseverance are intrinsically linked. While being patient with clients, we don't let them off the hook. We don't tell them they can take a year to solidify their recovery. They won't get more than ninety days in the best-case scenario, so we have to persevere in keeping clients moving gradually forward. It's up to us at Legacy Village—and I mean everyone from cafeteria attendants to doctors—to model perseverance within a framework of patience.

CHAPTER TWENTY-FOUR
Meaning & Purpose

O ne of the things that's unique about the Legacy Village model is our focus on giving clients something to look forward to, not just a new lifestyle where they must avoid past mistakes. The key to that is in helping them sort out their lives until they have a sense of purpose. As for me, I left my last rehab with a sense of purpose about transforming Brad's apartment building into a men's sober living facility, and that strong direction is really what saved me. I didn't just return home to the same nothing I had left behind. I returned to a new dream, a goal, a purpose that felt meaningful to me. My having that sense of purpose guided my wife back to me, as she, too, needed a focus outside of herself, so she got on board with my mine. In turn, that led to me giving myself an even higher goal to start a rehab center, and one thing led to another until I ended up here— successful and helping others be so, as well. It all started with what I now term: "meaning and purpose."

I feel like it's helpful to break down the newly recovered person's mindset into these two subsets in order to make sure they've got a foundation for success. Essentially, the "meaning" is the "why," as in: Why are we here? Why are we important? Why am I the way I am? It comes from more of a spiritual viewpoint. It can also be the "what," as in: What you're trying to achieve on the material plane? For instance, for me, when I first recovered (the third time) the new meaning of my life was to get my family back together, to be a good husband and father and friend to those (like Brad) who had helped me, and be a better son to my parents. That was the thing that would give my life meaning. It was the why and the what in my new life. When the clients at Legacy Village are ready to look at their futures, our therapists here try to help them determine what the meaning of that new life will be, so they have a deeply spiritually grounded reason to go on. Of course, there were practical concerns, too, such as how to make a living, how to get my family back together, and so forth, but that was just the technical to-do list of my life. It's important not to confuse life's practical concerns with the spiritual ones.

With a new *meaning* to life firmly established, clients can then decide what they're going to do with their newly sober selves in order to pursue that meaningful life, which is what I call their "purpose." If a man has uniting his family again as his life's meaning, then his purpose might include all the actions pertaining to that. Or if a man's *meaning* is to restore his professional reputation, then his purpose may tie into making amends in order to let his associates know he has turned over a new leaf. It's different for everyone, but I find it's helpful to identify both the reason for your new life and the goals you'll have because of that reason, as separate entities.

Those in the business world might recognize *meaning* and *purpose* as being similar to the *goals* and *tasks* they set in their professional lives, except that, in this case, the *meaning* should be like an uber-goal—a deeply spiritual goal for self-betterment, not a material-world goal. The *purpose*, then, is comparable to the material-world *goal* of a person in business. This is what you desire to achieve or do on the physical plane.

By the time alcoholics come to rehab, they often are not just suffering from a lack of resources, but they're in something very close to a suicidal or destitute state. For me, it was a matter of not really caring whether I lived or died, and I find that's a common feeling among rehab clients. In order to get you to live, make a living, and support the lives of your family members, we first have to get you to care about whether you live or die, in the first place. That's what the *meaning* and *purpose* are for. This part of our wellness program gets down to the bedrock of clients' lives. It's something everyone needs, really, not just alcoholics. For some, they get this bedrock at a religious institution, therapy session, or other deeply contemplative environment, but others never get it. Then there are those who once had it but have since lost it.

Combined, they form what we call the Journey to Recovery and Wellness, and this is where we progress from the more spiritual place where *meaning* resides and move into the practical reality of what you will actually do with the hours and days of your life. For me, when I finally recovered, my *purpose* was to build a men's sober living house. Once I had done it, I determined my new purpose was to build a rehab center. There is no end to the *purposes* someone can have, one after the other. Meanwhile *meanings* are less likely to change. These are deeply felt reasons for living, which are not necessarily tied to the actual day to day functioning of your practical life, but, with practice, they can become more and more so.

For me, since my recovery, my *meaning*, which is to become the best husband, father, son, and friend that I can be, has permeated my entire life. I could make it simpler by saying I just wanted to be a good human, but to say that implies I don't need anything other than willpower. As a Christian, I know that isn't true. In fact, nothing good lies within me except through my faith and reliance on Christ. It is something I think about daily, even hourly. When I make decisions as a CEO, as an American voter, as a property owner—in all the situations that seem to be unrelated to my family relationships, I ask myself if this will affect my personal relationships for better or worse. I wonder what example I'm setting for my children, what world I'm building for their future, what safeguards I'm putting into place for my aging parents, and how my wife (and mothers in general) will fare in the world I'm helping to build. I wonder what opportunities I may be creating (or destroying) for friends or potential friends—others like me.

Another thing I've done to fulfill my meaning is to use all the benefits I have as CEO of Legacy Village to ongoingly provide for my family and friends, as well as, of course, our clients. For me, "making amends" doesn't end when I've made apologies for bad deeds or paid back debts. It's a matter of sharing my good fortune now with those who shared with me at other times—over and above what I received from them, in the past.

I have used my success here to finally buy my parents a house of their own. In order to keep my sister and her family nearby, I was able to give her and my brother-in-law opportunities: my sister, as my office manager, and her husband, as the head of facilities. Part of what inspired the recent move to the Central Coast was the fact that two of my father's siblings live in this area, so the family is gradually reuniting, as a result. I now throw birthday and holiday parties at my new home, in order to provide a hub where everyone is welcome. Best of all, I've been able to see my friendship with Brad Wiedmann continue and be a source of true friendship that he can lean on during his difficult times. I wouldn't even be alive without Brad and his willingness to take a risk. The fact that we remain friends and I can now be there for him when he needs it is nothing less than a testimony to God's grace.

Owning a rehab facility is a situation fraught with spiritual peril, frankly, because so many of these facilities are run by people just trying to milk insurance companies for whatever they can get, even if that means kicking clients out before they've fully recovered. The way our current insurance system works, in this country, recidivism is key to profit for many rehab centers, while it is the absolute worst thing for clients. It can be very easy to run a rehab that is profitable but does very little good, as long as you can living with the moral failings required. Those that are not run with a spiritual focus, in my opinion, are doomed to crank out failure. Additionally, while most rehab centers are not run by recovering alcoholics themselves, I believe that for Legacy Village, the fact that we are helps tremendously.

Our work with veterans has been the key to enabling me to build the kind of wellness center that can really make a difference, but I wish all treatment facilities could run like Legacy Village. That is not a statement implying perfection but just saying that if any rehab center could duplicate the heart and passion we have here, it would be a game-changer. To make that happen, the insurance industry would have to profoundly change. Profoundly. It would have to understand deeply that alcoholism is a disease that affects not just the individual but the larger society, the economy, and every aspect of human health. This disease must be treated properly and thoroughly. You don't treat cancer by just popping in for a couple chemo treatments and hoping for the best, but that's how most insurance companies treat most alcoholics. Take it from me, "hoping for the best" is as meaningless to alcoholism as it is to cancer.

In too many cases, facilities like ours get the blame when clients failure to recover. In fact, insurance companies like to point our failures or punish facilities and clients alike for relapses. While I wholeheartedly believe improvements are needed across the industry, blaming the industry as whole is a bit irresponsible, too. Even with the best-made plans, best intentions, people fail. It is a sad reality of the world of addiction treatment. Yet, when failures exist in other areas of healthcare, we aren't so quick to blame the provider. If a diabetic enters the emergency room with a blood sugar of 400, the hospital stabilizes the patient, teaches them how to manage the disease, and gives them tools to support their condition. Sounds pretty similar to what we do. Yet, if the diabetic goes home, eats a package of Oreos chased by a milkshake, then promptly goes into a coma, no one questions the hospital's care! The same isn't true for addiction treatment, where we gain little of the praise and most of the brunt of blame.

CHAPTER TWENTY-FIVE

Redemption

I've written this book about my own experience as an alcoholic—and my experience building and owning Legacy Village—in order to make the point that I don't think anyone is irredeemable. I myself felt irredeemable many times, and for me it was that gift of a Bible and God's grace that brought me out of it. Actually, it was my wife Erica, my friend Brad, a kind nurse in detox who got me into my final rehab facility, the mystery man who left that Recovery Bible by my bedside ... a lot of entities were sent by God to contribute to my recovery and still contribute to my sobriety. Because of all of them, and the graces and mercies given by God, I am redeemed.

Everyone's path out of alcoholism (and drug addiction) is different. Even though we put people through a certain program at Legacy Village, in treatment, the way a veteran interprets the information they receive will always be unique. The way they reunite (or don't) with family members will vary from person to person. How addicts make amends is unique, too. There isn't one recipe for it. It's just something that has to be done as uniquely as the individuals themselves. As a facility, we embrace that. All twelve-steppers probably would agree that if you take those steps, you can truly redeem yourself. I agree. Despite my own affinity for the twelve-steps, we aren't married to them at the facility. In fact, we focus on a program that is really, truly unique to the veteran we are serving. Either way, working a program of positive change, in essence, is the key. So, if you're down and out—especially if you did it to yourself—don't despair. There is a place for you in this world. In fact, you probably have a much bigger role to play than you could ever imagine. It is those of us who have seen the very gates of Hell that have the brightest vision of Heaven.

I learned a lot about the power of God's grace from one particular client, actually. It was during the brief time period when we were serving the general public. She was a self-proclaimed Wiccan and very into reading tarot cards. She had her own spiritual viewpoint, which is fine from a recovery standpoint, but her beliefs did not include the notion of a higher power. In fact, her belief in tarot put her in the mindset that she *was* the higher power, that she could see into the future and control the outcomes of events, even more-so than an ordinary person.

Alcoholism is basically a disease about being a control freak—it all starts because you can't stand to just feel however you feel. You want to feel good all the time, so you use alcohol to get high and stay high. Eventually, because people are complex biochemical beings, not robots, that high turns into an incurable low, so you drink more in the mistaken belief that you can bring back the initial high you felt before your body chemistry changed from all that alcohol ingestion. So, this client was not only manifesting her control drama through alcoholism but also through her so-called spiritual practice, which taught her she was the one in control of every aspect of her life and future.

In order to recover, the very first thing alcoholics must do is admit they have no control over their disease. If they had control, after all, they would have simply stopped drinking before things got to the point of rock bottom. Admitting that things are out of your control, and you must appeal to a higher power for help, is central to the Alcoholics Anonymous ethos. Belief that something— be it the natural surroundings, a group, or a deity— has more power than you is crucial. There is no requirement for clients to believe in any particular God or prophet or religion, but I freely share when given the chance about what worked for me. Some veterans already have other ideas of a higher power, which is something that we respect. However, surrendering to whatever that is, is crucial to recovery, and this lady not only couldn't do it, but she also couldn't even understand what she was being asked to do. In layman's terms, she was obstinate.

Her rebellion against the recovery program was obvious in every interaction with her. She participated in abstaining from using alcohol but refused to surrender any other aspect of control of her mind, body, and life, which made her hard to live with, for starters, but also it was clear she wouldn't remain sober. Accepting one's lack of control over the disease is the very first step. She couldn't do even that, and this obstinacy persisted for forty-five days. I can relate, as I myself couldn't surrender either until my third rehab. I pretended to, but I was faking. Now that I was on the other side of that relationship, I saw how obnoxious it was to work with someone like that and I sent up a little apology to all the therapists who had to work with me back then.

One day, after she'd been in the program for forty-five days, I showed up to work at 7:30 or 8:00 am and she was waiting for me at the office door. I couldn't help but wonder, "What now? More complaints?" She wasn't the client I wanted to see first thing in the morning, that's for sure, but as I opened the door for her, I saw she was crying hysterically, so much so that it took some time for her to calm down enough to talk.

She said that the night before, she had finally gotten sick of the whole program. She didn't understand what was being asked of her and didn't believe in a higher power, anyway. She couldn't force herself to believe in something she just plain didn't believe in. I understood that, of course. Belief is something that's either there or not. It comes whenever it comes … if at all. She did want to get sober, though, and improve her life, and that's why she had been trying all this time, even though nothing had clicked. She became so angry, finally, that she cried out to the God she didn't believe in and said, "God! If you're real, you gotta tell me something, because I don't know. I don't know what I'm doing!"

"Then, as clear as I can hear my voice right now," she told me, "I heard God say, 'I'm real and I love you.' I broke down into tears … and I've been crying ever since."

She continued to bawl. It wouldn't stop. It was the most dramatic epiphany I've ever seen. It was like she'd been absolutely wrenched out of her old, cynical self and, like a newborn baby, was freaking out about existing in a whole new world, trying to figure out who she was, now. She eventually moved back to Texas, where she's from, and got involved in a church, there.

I tell this story as an example of how people tend to arrive at the point of belief in a higher power in their own time, in their own way. All we do here is expose them to the idea and the notion that surrendering control is essential to recovery. Once they realize it's really true, they come around in their own way, be it gradual or sudden.

That client has kept in touch with us over the years, which is how I know she was a success story. Follow-up like that has been essential to making Legacy Village the *village* that it is, not just another rehab clinic that takes your money and sends you on your way. I know how much I needed a community of like-minded souls when I was early in recovery. I still need it now. I had it when I lived in men's sober living, and it wasn't enough to keep me sober, but I've thought about that a lot. When I started dating Erica, I fell off the wagon, and all because I didn't know how to have a sober relationship. I didn't have anyone to teach me, and I was still mired in the secrecy of being an alcoholic. That is exactly what we try to eradicate by maintaining ongoing relationships with clients.

I tried living in a sober living house after my second rehab, but in the end, I rejected that community in favor of alcohol— something addicts do a lot. I never did get it back until I created another one here, at Legacy Village. So, while the sense of ongoing care and long-term friendship we provide is great for clients, it's also something I need for myself. I know our clients need both the services we provide and the community we offer, but I also need the clients more than they'll ever know. They are like-minded souls. Along with the members of my church, our clients are "my people." That's why we go out of our way for people who I know have nobody else.

We once had a fellow (for the sake of anonymity we'll call him John) who admitted with dual diagnosis issues including aggressive mental health problems along with his alcoholism. He had been homeless before coming to us, so he stayed for ninety days and did very well, but when it was time for him to go, he didn't have anyone or anywhere to take him in. I converted a spot for him to stay on the grounds until we could find him some housing, and he ended up sticking around for six or seven months. Finally, he went into a men's sober living home designed for veterans and did very well there.

Now, this fellow had a certain habit, which was to go to a local bar in order to dance. Technically, he shouldn't have been in that environment, but he didn't drink there, he just loved to get out on that dance floor and boogie. So, one evening, he went there as usual and a homeless man followed him in, fired two shots randomly into the bar, and killed him instantly. The homeless man then walked outside, sat on the pavement, and waited for the police to come and arrest him. It was the strangest, most random horror, almost as if he had been killed by a psychotic version of his former self.

The staff here had all grown quite fond of the fellow during the time he'd spent with us, so we were completely devastated. It was one of those situations where you feel like you've got to do something, but you don't know what. So, what we did was to pay for John's remains to be returned to Texas, where the fellow was from, and where his family lived. His family members, and the small-town church he'd grown up in, were touched by the loving attention at such a devastating time and glad they could provide him with a dignified funeral, knowing he had been loved.

Currently, Legacy Village only serves veterans, so I can't say this is, necessarily, the place for everyone in need of redemption. Having to turn anyone away has continued to be a nagging source of discomfort for me. That said, redemption isn't only needed by alcoholics. I look at my own family, going back through the generations—a father who made his share of mistakes, a paternal grandfather who did time for manslaughter, a paternal great grandfather who refused to take his grandchildren in when they were orphaned, my mother who tried to block my access to her own parents out of spite, maternal grandparents who kicked their only daughter out of her house with the same spiteful energy, and a truckload of cousins, second cousins, great aunts, and great uncles who won't reveal even more hidden truths about our family out of shame. We're no angels, any of us. But I truly believe that we can all be redeemed. If God shed his grace on me, he will surely do so for all humble supplicants who lay their troubles at His feet.

Redemption doesn't happen all at once. For me, it happened in increments. Every moment when I faced despair and was redeemed just a little bit brought me to where I am now. But in each of those cases, what I did was ask. I asked, at detox, for a solution to the fact that I knew I would drink again. A nurse found a rehab for me. I asked Erica to get sober and stay with me. Somehow—and to this day, neither of us really knows how she did it—this gift was given to me. Without knowing I was praying, I prayed in that last rehab for guidance, and someone left that Recovery Bible on my bedside table. I asked and I received.

Even that day when I stood on the balcony of my hotel, looking at those prostitutes, judging them—that was an answer to the question: "What is to become of me if I continue down this path?" which I'd been asking myself, daily. In the beginning, I asked God by wondering—what will become of me? What's the point of life? What is love? Why bother trying? and so forth. I didn't realize that wondering is just another way of praying—only without knowing who is supposed to answer the question.

After you've had experiences like mine, you eventually realize someone *is* listening to your wondering. You *do* get answers. You start to point your questions to God, and then the wondering turns into praying, but it's all the same thing, really. God is listening, either way. My life is a testament to that. When people ask questions, God gives answers, which means redemption is possible, really, for anyone.

I have written this book because I like to share my story, but I've been frustrated that the opportunities I've been given for public speaking don't allow for the full picture. In small groups, I feel I'm better able to share my story of redemption quite effectively, but I admit I'm greedy—greedy for spreading the word about redemption. In small settings, the full depth of the work God has done in my life is hard to convey. I want to reach more people, help more nonbelievers to believe, and help more addicts to recover. I have spoken to large groups in Celebrate Recovery meetings, but I find these opportunities somewhat stifling, as I like to speak off the cuff, and such meetings prefer to have speakers follow a pre-approved script. So, for now, I'm going to depend upon this book to get my message out. After all, I can attest to the fact that being in rehab is a great opportunity to get some reading done!

The way my life has turned around from an absolute near-death situation is, I think, a miracle. I can't claim credit for it. I have neither the good sense nor the business acumen to have made all this happen on my own. I had help from God, who worked through friends and strangers alike.

CHAPTER TWENTY-SIX

Ironing Money

When I was a young child, when my father was employed and living on the straight and narrow, he was always obsessed with keeping up appearances. In public, Janee and I had to be dressed right, act right, and conform to his idea of what proper children do. In this regard, he was impossible to please because, in truth, he didn't have much of an idea of what proper children do, having had such a topsy-turvy childhood, himself, in foster care. Nonetheless, Dad made sure we kept up the best standard of appearances he could muster— ironed money, and all. So, in a way, ironing money was a false thing he did to keep up appearances. But, on the other hand, it was also something that gave him hope that those appearances might one day be reality.

Ironically, Dad's own father, who had led a much more tragic and aimless life than Dad himself, had introduced him to the concept of ironing money. Grandpa Martin was a drunk who stumbled through life until he stumbled in and out of prison, then stumbled onto a busy highway where, when he was killed. I'm going to assume they found his wallet full of perfectly crisp, ironed bills, if he had any. He hadn't ever given up on trying to have one good, pure, unbroken thing about himself. The only thing about him that was right, in the end, was that wallet full of crisp bills. But, to me, having those ironed bills meant he never gave up on himself. Even though circumstances led my grandfather to a dire fate, my father kept the same ironed-money philosophy, and he did better.

Growing up with teenaged parents means growing up together. Like any kid, Dad went through his respectable phase, then his degenerate phase. He went through a wild, unfaithful phase and, later, a phase of incredible gratitude and faithfulness to Mom, who stuck with him through it all. I'm not suggesting women have any obligation to do that with such men, but in the long run, my mother knew Dad was, for a long time, still a child testing his limits in the world. She understood that their love for each other—which they had both given up so much to fulfill— was a lifelong thing much stronger than each others' mistakes.

So, on the one hand, "ironing money" is one little thing you can do to give yourself hope, to remind yourself that there is a part of you that is good, crisp, unbroken—like that time in Bakersfield that I went to one single church service. That's where I met people, complete strangers, who believed I wasn't irredeemable. They ironed the little bit of spiritual money I had. In so doing, they gave me a spark of hope that the tiny, unbroken parts of me could grow and become a bigger part of who I was. On the other hand, ironing money can be a foolish act of trying to appear as something you're not. If your spiritual gains are ill-gotten—if you're faking your belief in a higher power, if you're pretending to care about your community, if you're imitating a sober person even as you spend weekends getting loaded—then you're creating a false impression of crispness that will soon become rumpled, again. Most addicts go through both of these phases and more. They're sincere but also insincere. They're disciplined but also chaotic. They maintain hope, but often for a selfish objective. In either case, we're all ironing our money in one way or another, most of the time. I just hope that I, and the clients at Legacy Village, can keep on doing it for the right reasons. I hope that for anyone who reads this story.

What we do, though, in helping addicts, is just one small aspect of what, I feel, needs to happen in America's larger society. Of course, not everyone is an alcoholic or drug addict, so not everyone wrestles with the same demons, but the same tendencies manifest in innumerable ways. In the larger world, you have obese people who are addicted to food, fit people who are addicted to working out, well-educated perfectionists addicted to high achievement, and hard workers addicted to acquiring money as an aim in itself. You've got social media users addicted to their own images, young adults addicted to a search for sexual fulfillment to the exclusion of other types of fulfillment. It's important, I think, for people to realize how unhealthy these obsessions are.

For me, having a strong, guided relationship with God has been the thing that led me out of that tunnel-vision mindset and helped me see that, as part of a community, the more I give, the better my life is. The more I obsess on my own needs, desires, and ambitions, the less fulfilled I ultimately am. This is the message of Christianity. It is the message of recovery. It is the anti-addiction mindset. It is the humble mindset of self-as-part-of-community, not the proud mindset of self-as-savior-of-mankind. The concept of holistic wellness we teach here at Legacy Village is something I hope catches on in the wider world, which needs this viewpoint so much. It also requires personal responsibility. You have to own your actions and the consequences before you can move forward. We call that acceptance.

A lot of people these days are even addicted to categorizing themselves—in an attempt to escape the standard, old-fashioned categorization of man/woman, boy/girl, son/daughter, husband/wife which they see as constricting and inaccurate, they spend unheard-of amounts of brain power, free time, and money on publicly recategorizing themselves as nonbinary/bisexual/asexual/gay/ trans/ transitioning/polyamorous and so forth. Creating a unique identity seems to be the latest addiction for Americans. I say it's an addiction because in many cases friends and lovers are won and lost based upon the absolute intensity and importance of these identities in some peoples' lives. Failure to accept someone and refer to that person with the correct terms to indicate the new categorization is often seen as a betrayal on the deepest level— that's how important these categorizations are to these types of addicts. The spiritual part of me looks at this social trend and sees a giant hole in the logic.

God, after all, doesn't categorize people in that way. God accepts all of us, with our imperfections, unusual qualities, quirky tendencies, strange obsessions, and oddball habits. In God's eyes, nobody is excluded from the right to serve others, be part of a community, give of oneself, express gratitude, and seek a higher purpose. Ironically, it is the lack of a spiritual compass, a lack of God, that leads to these identify crises. I think if people thought less about "being themselves" they'd think more about serving others, and their happiness would, in that way, manifest in a deeper way than any superficial categorization—whether traditional or innovative—could fulfill.

Addiction is the mindset of any control freak. Alcoholics and drug addicts are obsessed with controlling their moods, so they take whatever uppers or downers are needed to make them feel the way they want to feel. They can't accept that life will dole out happiness and depression in its own way, and one must find a way to roll with the circumstances. Sure, being happy in life is partly about controlling one's circumstances—you don't want to go broke, so you work to control the contents of your bank account, for instance. You can't just leave everything up to God and not lift a finger. If I'd done that, I'd still be starving to death on Pismo Beach. But control is a dance. When tragedy strikes, when accidents change your life, when injustice robs you of what's yours, when the world doesn't give you what you deserve, when gambles don't pay off—you have to accept that control has been wrested from you, and then you have to trust that God will make things right. It helps to look at anything, Legacy Village for example, as something God has given me stewardship over. It isn't mine, it's on loan – and being a good steward of what I've been given is required. Believing in a higher power is exactly what has enabled me to get through the hard times in building Legacy Village. I didn't know what I was doing most of the time, but I trusted that if I was on the right path, things would work out. That's a lot of belief. That's a lot of surrender. If Legacy Village had gone bust and all my efforts went down the drain, I would have had to admit that it had been the wrong path for me. I'm glad that didn't happen, but I've traveled a lot of wrong paths in my life, and, ultimately, with each one, I had to face it, steer myself down a different, unknown path, and try again. Those are the moments when I broke out of my control-freak mindset and accepted the world as it was.

But, I admit, each time, I waited until the point of absolute desperation to do it.

Operating as a recovered alcoholic and a (mostly) non-control-freak means relinquishing control of life to God *before* the point of absolute desperation. Doing this is easier when people accept their personal responsibilities—something modern Americans seem to have a hard time with, indeed. For instance, during those years when I was drinking to live and living to drink, I thought very little about my parents, my kids, and what effect I was having on those around me. I had no sense of responsibility, just a quest for personal pleasure. It's no wonder, though— in American society at large, the quest for personal pleasure and ego fulfillment is celebrated as if it's the holy grail. Young people are taught that their primary aims should be making money, fulfilling sexual desires, having fun, and building their "brand." In fact, the notion that family and community come before one's personal desires is often seen as oppressive and invalidating of one's personal identity. The patriarchy strikes again! Just speaking from my own experience, I have found that once I surrendered to serving God, serving my fellow addicts, and doing what I, in my heart, knew to be morally and ethically right, everything I selfishly wanted was showered down upon me.

Now, we live comfortably. Now, Erica and I have most of our extended family living close together and we're parenting our kids and giving back to our parents. Now, my wife and I have a great relationship. Now, I live in a beautiful home and enjoy the luxury of free time and hobbies. In a way, I'm just plain lucky. If the VA had never called and made its offer to me, I would never be here, today. But the reason they did call me and make that offer was because addicts went through my program and started talking about how this place was different. It was being run by a guy who actually *gave a shit* (to use a very non-spiritual but entirely accurate phrasing). When you do the right thing for the right reason, it's unusual. People notice. You stand out as a point of light in a dark world, and that is so incredibly meaningful to people who have been consumed by the darkness both within and without. It also doesn't hurt to have God opening doors, and that requires faith, surrender, and patience.

In a way, taking personal responsibility for a community instead of just the self fulfills selfish goals. It seems counter-intuitive, though. After all, this is like looking at the big red balloon you want and, instead of reaching for it, you walk the opposite direction. You can only do that if you understand the world is round and you'll come back around to that balloon in time, and it will be so much better when you do. You have to have faith that the long path is the right path, and you can only see that if either:

1. you have no other choices (that's how I ended up here)

   or

2. you've seen others do it, so you've learned the truth of life vicariously.

That's what I'm trying to do with this book—help you (addict or not) understand that walking away from selfishness is the path to fulfilling your desires. I hope you can learn this the easy way, instead of the hard way I had to go through. I hope you can surrender to God and to service, reap the rewards of that lifestyle, and make this world a better place for us all, sooner rather than later. It isn't like I'm perfect at it – but I try again, every day. For my dad, it took a long time. In a way, having me was the key to that. Everything he put me through led to everything I put myself through, but ultimately, it led to both of us coming out of the darkness, together. It kind of seems predestined. If I'd never been born, would Dad have ever found peace in his soul? That question can't be answered, but I'm glad he had the contented, peaceful, fulfilled ending that he did. My father died on February 24, 2023, just before I finished writing this book, but he was a changed man by then. His spiritual money was naturally crisp. It didn't even need to be ironed.

What follows is the eulogy I wrote for Dad, but it's more than one man's story. It's a tale about how the struggle to survive and thrive provides people with the incredible opportunity to find fulfillment through service. His life is a story about forgiveness of others, of self, and believing that we are all redeemable. Every one of us. All the time.

CHAPTER TWENTY-SEVEN

Eulogy for Orville Scott Farmer

ost of us have seen death before, at least those of us old enough
to have lost grandparents, aunts, or uncles. Some of us have lost
friends too soon. Losing a parent, I am learning, is a different
experience altogether. For most of us, parents are the closest, most intimate
person we will ever lose, other than a spouse. We think we know them, or,
at least, know them as well as any person can know another. But what I
have been surprised about is just how much we didn't know about Dad.
His death has reminded me of the things we have been taking for granted,
especially during the outpourings of support, well wishes, and condolences
since Dad passed.

Dad was a man who never met a stranger that didn't become a friend.
I already knew that, but then came the stories. For some context, Dad
was late to his own wedding because he stopped to change a stranger's
tire alongside the highway. That pattern would continue for his entire
life. In fact, a former client of our facility wrote a message after Dad's
passing. It seems he had run into Dad in the mall in Bakersfield. (First,
no idea what Dad was doing in the mall!) Dad asked the client what he
was doing there, and after explaining he was shopping for a ring for his
wife, Dad pulled $200.00 from his pocket and handed it over. Despite
repeated objections, Dad insisted, and everyone knows how that works,
when Dad would insist. More likely than not, Dad didn't have an extra
$200.00, either.

Dozens more messages like that one came through, thanking us—Mom, Janee, and me—for sharing Dad with everyone. Another story recounted Dad's frequent habit of picking people up – God only knows what time of day or night – without asking where you were going, what time you would be back, or what you would be doing. You were expected to get in the truck with no questions asked.

Other stories recounted early morning cups of coffee with healthy doses of advice … followed by more advice. There was never a shortage of advice from Dad.

I started trying to write this eulogy while we were still sitting with Dad in the final days, and much of what I have to say was inspired by the messages, texts, and Facebook posts that overwhelmed us all with a sense of pride, hope and gratitude. Other parts were inspired by Dads' own words. He began writing things down when he first suspected he had cancer in his eye.

January 7, 2019: He wrote, "No doubt I am facing the fear of death after going to get my eyes checked. Doc says he believes there is a tumor or blood blocking my vision in the right eye. Reading everything I can find, it doesn't look good. I hope and, believe me, PRAY it is something other than cancer." He went on to say, "People have always told me I'm too ornery to die in the same age group my other siblings have. Man, I hope they're right. If it turns out to be cancer, they say that 80% get to live an additional five years. I'll sure take it and be glad to get it." Dad didn't make it the five years, but he did make it four – and, man, those four years were full. True to his words, he exhibited gladness for every moment of it.

Later, in that same journal entry, he said, "But, no matter, I am going to try my best to live whatever time is left as grateful and giving as I can. I hope it's not too late to start praying because I am starting. I don't believe anyone except God can keep me sane through this." He spent the last four years as grateful for the time as anyone I've ever known. And he knew where to place his struggles – with God. Two days later, he had confirmation. It was cancer. He was scared. He ended his passage on

January 9, 2019, with "Let me say I'm turning this problem over to God. That's right, God. It's too big for me."

Dad certainly wasn't easy to get along with all the time. He could be stubborn and downright difficult. In his view, he wasn't always right, but he was *never* wrong. In short, he was complicated at times, and in a lot of ways, especially when it came to faith.

I started trying to write this at Mom and Dad's kitchen table, but in some respects, I've been writing this in my mind ever since we knew the day of Dad's death was approaching. Writing your father's eulogy is kind of a rite of passage, a time where, as the oldest child, you're left to reassure those around you that his memory, his wishes, and his life lessons will continue. Even before he passed, I began to take mental notes during the one-on-one conversations Dad and I would have, most of which happened during our weekly forty-five-minute trips to the casino.

He loved our casino trips, and towards the end, many of those were just he and I. As the reality of the situation set in, these conversations became more meaningful. He shared about his wishes, his hopes for a time after he would be gone. He talked about mistakes, and he talked about success. And, not unlike most other times, he had questions.

He wanted to know why. Dad always wanted to know why. Why had he lost his Mom so early? Why did he grow up in such difficult circumstances? Why had his grandfather passed in an accident, instead of peacefully in his sleep? Why, why, why. We would talk about the "why" of so many things, the inevitable question of "why" he was here, or "what" was it all for came to the front. What impact did he have? What was the purpose of this chaotic journey? We talked a lot about family, too. It seemed to be the answer he was always returning to. And, in the moments where he searched desperately for meaning, we talked about faith, which is interesting because his need to know why, his questioning, was the thing that prevented Dad, much of his life, from embracing any relationship with God.

Dad grew up in church. In fact, he was the grandson of an Assembly of God pastor, but the circumstances of his young life caused him great doubt and led to all these unanswerable questions. Then, when he was an adult, things continued to go sideways. In fact, I would be remiss in acting as if Dad's life went according to any plan at all. Our family, in some form or another, has fallen apart and been brought back together more than once. We talked about that on those drives, too.

It was Pastor Dennie who was with him last year when something finally allowed for a re-acceptance of God and Jesus Christ as his savior. We know now, after reading his journal, the embers for that faith were already being rekindled long before that conversation. There weren't flashes of lightning or thunder when Dad and Pastor Dennie prayed, although I'm certain even God was wondering if he'd ever come around. But that's the beauty of God's mercies and grace. It may have taken a moment to get there, but a small opening was all He needed.

Dad prayed with Pastor Dennie that day, as he would do many more times until the end, and then he promptly resumed asking, "Why?" And that's okay. God doesn't mind us asking questions. He doesn't mind us getting emotional, as long as we're talking to Him. And Dad did, albeit with language that would raise an eyebrow from time-to-time. The reason for the passage we chose in the memorial program is to remind us that even at the last moments, we can call out to Jesus – and despite our stubbornness, despite our wayward journeys, He remains faithful to his word, and He is there for us.

Dad had a way of creating moments with each of us – he always did, but they were especially prominent in the last months. I don't know if it was intentional or if it just came naturally, but nonetheless there were moments— moments we knew we would never recapture, but we would also never forget, moments we knew were important, even though we acted as if we were in casual conversation. This was Dad's way of making sure the seeds were planted, and his wishes, hopes, and dreams were memorialized.

We talked, too, about Dads childhood. Dads' life as a child would be something that both haunted him and drove him forward. It would be the defining factor, I believe, in what is and will continue to become, his legacy. His past would be in the demons he battled and the triumphs he enjoyed. And so it is with the struggles of life: we can allow them to cripple us with fear, plague us with addictions, and strangle us with regrets, or we can use them as tools and motivation towards a better, stronger, and more resilient future, enabling us to pass lessons to the next generation.

Over time, Dad's life saw both demons and triumphs. We talked about that, too, on those casino drives, which seemed to pass by too quickly, now. Nearer to the end, when the questions about his purpose were not just to himself but to God, answers came more clearly. He didn't really have to say that, though. You could tell, as a peace about his situation fell upon him.

It is hard to define the clarity of what Dad began to see. I think he found clarity in his role in this life. I think he found certainty in the impact he had on others. I am assured that today he knows every answer to every question. Those of us who survive him remain limited in what we can understand, and only when our own time has come will we know the true masterpiece of God's design. But I think what Dad discovered was that his life was about <u>being</u> the change he so desperately wanted to see. He understood that praying for a close family and wishing for con-nection to others doesn't simply make it so. You have to actively partici-pate. You have to make the conscious choice to be an agent of change.

The last years of Dad's life were probably the most profound, especially in respect to being a catalyst for change. The fifty-five years prior to this were just practice. The hurts, the hang-ups, the love, and the loss were all preparation for those last years, when his harsh approach to everything softened and when, with each passing year, the scolding lectures became wise advice. The anger became concern. The hurt became empathy. The sadness became opportunity. The mistakes and missteps became hope.

Through Dad's work at Legacy Village, he would see others (perhaps he saw them as younger versions of himself) and in a way <u>no trained person could</u>, he would share in their concern. He loved the clients and staff at Legacy in a way that few of us can imagine. Dad genuinely cared for people from every walk and every circumstance in life. He honestly could empathize; he showed them opportunity and he offered them hope—not the kind of empty words that we so often hear but hope from the mouth of someone who clearly had been there. It gave him credibility.

In his family, Dad let the anger of the past go, and with sincerity showed unconditional love. When he told any of us he understood, he did. He also both created and took advantage of every opportunity to show us this unquestionable sincerity. Through the trips, parties, events, and more, he showed us the benefits of hope, for when we were all together, we experienced the joy only a thing hoped for can produce.

Mom, you saw all the stages of Dad, from almost the beginning. We talked about that, too, on those drives, which, each week, became ever more precious than before. He loved you in a way that gives all of us reason to smile. He remained, until the very end, in awe of you. He was in awe that over the years, through the many tears and even more laughter, you remained steadfast by his side. He remained in awe of you, for who you are, for your role as a wife, mother, grandmother, and friend. He was in awe that he somehow managed to have you by his side. Being your husband was by far the thing he was most proud of. He rarely was able to say that out loud, though. He chose, more often, to give you a hard time, instead. It was his way. But I'm certain in the quiet moments you shared, he told you as much. And on those occasions where no sarcasm could be found, he shared it with us, too.

I know he was proud of both Janee and me, but he reserved being the second most proud of his grandkids and of being Papa. To his grandkids:

Haley, you were the first, and how you survived being babysat by Papa for as long as you did still baffle most of us. He loved you so much, and he began to change for the better the moment you were born. You taught him how to be a grandpa. He loved you even more than you know. Watching you grow into a beautiful young woman was one of the greatest joys of his life.

Leila, he adopted you as a granddaughter the moment he met you. He found a partner in crime not afraid to drive a go-cart or pull a trailer with his pickup … even before you had a license. He loved you, and I'm sure he'll being trying to set you up with the right date from Heaven. He was proud to watch you grow up and proud to be your papa.

Kelsy, Papa had a special place in his heart for you. He saw a lot of Nani and your mother in you, and he wasted no time telling anyone about your talent in softball and how proud he was. He loved you, and when the next homerun makes it out of the park, and it shouldn't have, maybe it was him with a little assist.

Brody, watching you grow into a young man was one of the joys of his life. He was so proud to watch you play sports, and even more excited to give you tips and advice. He loved you very much. The time the two of you spent talking wrestling in the living room during Christmas was really special to him, and he talked about it more than once. It was time that just the two of you got to share.

Anthony, you're his namesake. It wasn't lost on Papa that it is left to you to carry on the Farmer name. He was so proud of you. He thought you were smart but didn't want to say it because he didn't want it to go to your head. You get that intelligence from him. Watching the two of you argue because you each thought you knew something was always funny to me, because you got that from him, too. I can assure you, however, he was right. Trust me, I've been there.

Alyssa, it took you a while to warm up to Papa, and he knew that, and he was okay to give you time. When you spent time with him on our last trip to the river, and played Aggravation – game-after-game - you made him so happy. He was so proud of the young lady you are becoming.

Emily, you were the youngest. You were the baby, and you got to avoid most of the lectures the rest of the grandkids had to endure … from the time he put a motorcycle helmet on you when you were less than year old, to digging a giant hole on the beach, he was smiling from ear to ear. He loved you and was proud of you.

His hope for all of you is that you'll work to keep his legacy going. And what is that legacy? The talks, the drives, the lessons, the lectures, the advice— what did it all add up to? What answers did he find before he left us? What legacy is being left to the seven of you, his grandchildren, to uphold, build upon, and continue?

Love.

Dad, Papa, loved bigheartedly, even when it was hard. In good times and bad, he loved. He loved his family. He loved his friends. He loved people. Even when it was hard.

Generosity.

Dad didn't always have much, but with what he had he was generous. Your papa would give without expecting anything in return. He gave money, he gave his talents, and most of all he gave his time. He would sit and talk with anyone – and I mean anyone. It's a skill we all should learn.

Respect.

When your papa last saw his own father, they fought. It stayed with him his entire life. It is why, regardless of circumstance, he railed against ever staying mad at someone. But that wasn't always how Papa acted. In fact, he held a grudge much of his younger life. With time, however, and life experience, he valued and respected others. He realized that every person is sometimes battling something we know nothing about. He realized that sometimes we respect those older than us for no other reason than they're older. He realized that sometimes we respect those older because they've been there.

Faith.

Your papa didn't always talk about faith very easily. But he had faith. And while it wasn't always faith in God, he still practiced faith. He had faith in other people, in the goodness that we all have in us. He had faith in the ability others have to do wonderful, amazing things. He had faith in the ability YOU have to do wonderful, amazing things. He had faith in the impact that Love, Generosity, and Respect would have in this world. And yes, faith in God, too. Which, by far, is the most important thing you could learn from him.

He always knew that there is something more than the world that we see around us. While it took him longer to gain some acceptance of that, you don't have to wait that long. Our hope to see him again lies solely in faith— faith that Jesus died on the cross for all of us, faith that Dad accepted that fact, and faith that we, too, will accept the same. Our job—mine and Erica's, and, Janee, you and Tony, too—is to carry on his example the best we can, sharing with our kids those qualities about Dad we don't ever want forgotten. That's how memories are preserved and legacies are defined.

Dad reserved for only two women (that I know of) the utmost respect and regard. One, of course, was Mom. The other was his Aunt Ruenell. When it came to compassion, faith, being honorable and sincere, and when it came to class and how a person carried themselves, there was none as special as Aunt Ruenell to Dad. He very much loved you and treasured the last times you were able to visit. Throughout the years, you were the closest he had to a mother, and he cherished that.

Dad also loved his brothers and sisters. Over the past years, he was able to spend the most time with two of them. Aunt Marlene, he so enjoyed being your bigger brother and reminding you he was smarter and wiser. He enjoyed that he was a part of your life, and he enjoyed giving you a hard time. He enjoyed reminding you to be nice to David and David, he loved you like a brother. Uncle Bill, the two of you argued so much, I'm sure, because you both enjoyed arguing so much. Half the time, I don't think there was ever really a disagreement. In the last years, you two became closer than ever, so through all of the ups and downs you came together when it counted. I know you and he were both better because of it. He loved you, he respected you, and he trusted you. Aunt Shirley, we all know Uncle Bill is so wonderful because of you, and Dad knew that, too. He loved you like his own sister.

We would be here far too long – and far longer than Dad would like – if I took the time to speak to everyone who was impacted, or who had an impact, on his life. There were many. And there are many more stories like I began with, some we know and many which we may never know.

Dad didn't brag about his charity and he didn't gossip about the help he gave.

Knowing death is coming is an interesting experience, and in some respects more forgiving. He had to endure the pain and illness associated with his cancer, and the emotional rollercoaster that would come, but he also had time. Precious time. Time to say things he wanted to say, do things he wanted to do, and reconcile with the past before it was too late.

Not all of us will get that opportunity. Driving late at night on our weekly casino trip, we talked about that, as well. The drive, by now, seems to have passed in minutes. We talked about things Dad would never have said before – meaningful things, heartfelt things, things that mattered.

Dad spent his final months, then weeks, then days, visiting with family and friends, some close and some long-lost, who he'd found his way to reconnecting with. He smiled and grinned at the marvel of a new life when my cousin Jake brought his baby Ruby to the house. Maybe he was smiling because of something funny she had done, or maybe he was smiling because he knew a piece of his brother, Smokey, would be in that little girl, and that made Dad happy.

It always made Dad happy to know a memory would live on. I once complained to him of the volume of pictures being acquired and the difficulty of managing them all, to which I was promptly reprimanded, "There are NEVER too many pictures." He was right, and in moments like this we realize we want more.

He relished giving my cousin Tony a hard time on the dunes in Pismo and running him ragged as if to squeeze every moment from every minute of time. He did that a lot at the end. He embraced every moment of living life to its fullest. He didn't slow down till he had to. He looked at his cousin Marty with acceptance, rather than argument, when asked if his salvation was secured. He squeezed his hand to confirm it. Gone was the bitterness or uncertainty and left was peace.

I would also not be able to give this message without acknowledging all of you here, affectionately known, as the moose family. Of all the changes made with moving from Bakersfield to the coast, Mom and Dad's joining the moose lodge was one of the most positive and rewarding.

There, they found friendship, fun and a sense of belonging. They found new members of the Farmer family. Dad truly loved all of you and was overwhelmed with the outpouring of support you showed during his illness. At the moose lodge, among his family, he was at home. You all have a dear and special place in the heart of our family. You're a part of our family, and for everything, thank you. Dad spent his final time on earth telling everyone who would listen, and a few who wouldn't, how important these connections are. Connection to family and to friends – even to strangers.

He could see that with more clarity than ever, too. When it mattered, when the end was near, that was ALL that mattered. Dad came from generations that, not for lack of trying, left this world with their immediate families in turmoil. He longed for his own family to stay united, to be close, and to share in the sadness and gladness of life, together. He left this world with that hope, that desire, that legacy, accomplished.

He used the time he had to share a love and a wisdom that only the dying can share. He had the complete honesty that only those facing their mortality can have. It was raw, unfiltered, and blunt – and it was the truth. We take nothing with us when we leave this world. No riches, no possessions, not even this vessel we use to walk the earth. We do, however, leave <u>behind</u> a great deal. We leave much for those whose journey and whose work are not yet done.

Dad knew what he was leaving behind. He had shown all the love he had to give. He had given all the wisdom he had to share. He had said the things needing to be said and took with him the secrets only a friend would know. Dad hung out with sinners and saints, although I'm sure he preferred the sinners, not because he enjoyed the wayward life, but because he saw in <u>everyone</u>, what many of us frequently miss --- a person. He saw the best in people, even when all odds were against them. He saw the value they had. Maybe it was a trait from his grandpa Farmer. Maybe it was his own experience of feeling discarded. Maybe it was the gift God gave him to share. <u>Maybe it was all three</u>.

You never know what events will transpire in your life to lead you to any given moment. You never know what souls you'll encounter along the way. This entire world would be a better place if we all practiced a little of what Dad brought to the world … but that's a pretty tall order. I think he'd settle for knowing those of us in this room would practice it a little more. Practice a little more love and little less judgment. Practice a little more generosity and little less self-indulgence. Practice a little more respect and little less ego. And practice a little more faith … in God and in others.

Next time you see a stranger, make them a friend. Next time, accept that invitation. Next time, make that phone call. Next time, take that trip. Next time, listen to that story. Don't respond, just listen. Next time, listen to that advice. It may hurt, but it's worth it. Next time, take that chance. On that inevitable day when there are no more 'next times,' you'll be grateful you did.

Maybe, just maybe, in that moment, when you can say you've lived life to its fullest and left nothing to chance, you'll think of Dad and smile. That my friends, is a legacy. It's the legacy of my father. It's the legacy of a husband, a grandpa, a brother, a cousin, and a friend. It is the Legacy of Orville Scott Farmer.

It feels fitting to end the book on this note that is recognizing Dad's legacy but also bringing full circle what this work is trying to accomplish. After all, we are all working on what will become our own legacy. "Next time" is just another way of saying: take that opportunity, the opportunity to be kind, helpful, caring and patient. Or "next time" can mean take that chance, ask that girl out on a date, ride the roller coaster. Whatever "next times" you find yourself faced with, know that the day will come when there will be no more. When that day comes, and you can say that you did for others, gave credit to someone or something other than yourself, found God, and survived it all. That, too, is a legacy. Your own.